The Path to Glory

**THE HISTORY OF
BLACK APOSTOLIC ORGANIZATIONS
& THE PIONEERS THAT SHAPED THE MOVEMENT**

Bishop Cornelius Showell

Seymour Press ˢP

Lanham, MD

The Path to Glory

Copyright © 2022 Cornelius Showell

All rights reserved. No parts of this book may be reproduced in any form without written permission from Seymour Press.

All images are in the public domain.

Printed in the United States of America.

ISBN: 9781938373923
LCCN: 2024942307

*It shall be light in the evening time
The path to glory you will surely find
Thru the water way;
It is the Light today.
Buried in His precious name,
Young and old repent of all your sins,
Then the Holy Ghost will enter in.
The evening time has come;
Tis a fact that God and Christ are one.*

Hattie Pryor
1919

This book is dedicated to
Bishop Joseph Morsel Turpin
Mother Ruth Beatrice Turpin
Bishop Winfield Amos Showell
Mother Genevieve Frances Showell

CONTENTS

Forward i

Introduction 1

Part One – Organizations and Fellowships

    Pentecostal Assemblies of the World 7

    Church of God (Apostolic) 13

    Apostolic Faith Mission Church of God 15

    Apostolic Overcoming Holy Church of God 17

    Emmanuel Tabernacle Baptist Church 19

    Church of Our Lord Jesus Christ 21

    Glorious Church of God in Christ 25

    The Churches of God and True Holiness 27

    Way of the Cross Church of Christ 29

    Church of the Lord Jesus Christ 31

    Zion Gospel Churches of the Apostolic Faith 33

    Highway Christian Church of Christ 34

    Apostle Church of Christ in God 35

    Progressive Church of Our Lord Jesus Christ, Inc. 37

    Church of God in Jesus Christ (Apostolic) 39

    Original Glorious Church of God in Christ 41

    Highway Churches of Christ 43

    Pentecostal Churches of the Apostolic Faith 44

    Bible Way Church of Our Lord Jesus Christ 46

    Bible Way Pentecostal Apostolic Church 49

    Greater Emmanuel International Fellowship 50

    True Vine Pentecostal Churches of Jesus 51

Free Gospel Churches of the Apostles' Doctrine 52
Apostolic Inter-Organizational Fellowship 53
Living Witness of the Apostolic Faith.................................... 54
Mount Hebron Apostolic Temple 55
Holy Temple Church of the Lord Jesus Christ..................... 56
United Church of Jesus Christ (Apostolic)............................ 57
Cainhoy Miracle Revival Corporation 58
Apostolic Assemblies of Christ... 59
United Churches of Jesus, Apostolic...................................... 60
Refuge Temple Assembly of Yahweh 61
Church of Jesus Christ Apostolic, Inc.................................... 62
Evangelistic Churches of Christ 63
United Way of the Cross of the Apostolic Faith 63
Alliance of Apostolic Churches of Christ Jesus..................... 65
Holy Temple Church of Christ 66
Redeemed Assembly of Jesus Christ, Apostolic.................... 66
National Apostolic Fellowship Association 67
Higher Ground Always Abounding Assemblies.................... 68
Beth-El Churches of Christ 69
World Assemblies of Restoration 70
Apostolic Faith Fellowship International............................... 71

Part Two – Pioneers and Leaders

William Charles Abney 75
Joseph H. Adams... 77
Elmer Fremont Akers 79
J. W. Ardrey... 80
George W. Ayers 81
Oddous Barber 83

John D. Barnes	84
William S. Barnes	85
Ralph Bass	86
Sidney Coy Bass	87
John Solomon Beane	88
D. Rayford Bell	89
Isaiah W. Bollinger	90
Ethel Mae Bonner	91
William Lee Bonner	93
George Marshall Boone	95
Frank Reuben Bowdan	97
Maggie Bowdan	99
Paul Alexander Bowers	100
Bernard Nathaniel Bragg	101
Arthur Monroe Brazier	103
Peter J. F. Bridges	105
George Harold Brooks	107
Henry Chauncey Brooks	109
John Luke Brooks	111
Henry H. Brown	112
Ramsey Nathaniel Butler	113
Lucille Tanzella Calloway	114
Randolph Adolphus Carr	115
William A. Carson	117
Dunlap Chenault	118
James I. Clark Sr.	119
David Collins	121
George Cooke	122
Thomas J. Cox	123

William Crossley 124

Aletha June Cushinberry 125

Belle Davis 126

Hebert Davis 127

Raymond Fox Davis 128

Riley Marcilous Davis 129

Nah William Dixon 131

Robert Oliver Doub 132

Anna Belle Douglas 133

Floyd Ignatius Douglas 135

Sydney Alexander Dunn 137

Harry Clay Eggleston 139

Robert Evans Jr. 140

Isabell Brooks Ford 141

Lillian Ford 142

John Wesley Garlington, Jr. 143

John Wesley Garlington, Sr. 145

William Gerald 146

Morris Ellis Golder 147

B. J. Goode 149

Randolph Goodwin 150

Simon Tenyen Grant 151

Ralph E. Green 152

Martin Rawleigh Gregory 153

Samuel Joshua Grimes 155

Kathleen (S.K.) Grimes 157

Isaiah Warren Hamiter 159

Samuel Nathan Hancock 160

Gladstone Theophilus Harewood 162

Thoro Harris	163
Garfield Thomas Haywood	165
Ida Haywood	168
John Silas Holly	169
Aaron James Holmes	170
Pearl Julia Holmes	170
Ellen Moore Hopkins	171
W. O. Howard	172
Lenist J. Hunter	173
Maurice H. Hutner	174
Lulu Jackson	175
Norma Sylvester Jackson	176
James Archie Johnson	177
Lymus Leewood Johnson	179
Margaret Giles-Johnson	181
Sherrod Charlotte Johnson	183
Pearl Williams Jones	185
Robert Clarence Lawson	187
Austin Augustus Layne	191
Samuel Austin Layne	193
Clester Richard Lee	194
Willie Lee	195
George Grover Levant	196
Susan Gertrude Lightford	197
Lillian Mason	199
Robert James McGoings	200
Robert William McMurray	201
Marian B. Miller	203
Mary E. Mills	204

Benjamin Thomas Moore	205
Clarence E. Moore	206
Joseph Moore	207
James Thomas Morris	208
Eli N. Neal	209
Floyd Edward Nelson	210
Earl Parchia	212
James Walter Parrott	213
Joseph Paulceus	214
John W. Pernell	215
Delphia Perry	216
B. D. Pettiford	217
Emma Heil Pettiford	217
Otho Pettiford	218
Lulu Lightey Phillips	219
William Thomas Phillips	221
Charles Edward Poole	223
Mattie Belle Poole	223
Henry Prentiss	225
Hattie E. Pryor	227
Viola Redd	228
Jeremiah Reed	229
Hilda Reeder	231
James C. Richardson	233
Jasper Roby	235
Sylvia Rose	237
Nina Ryan Russell	239
Oscar Haywood Sanders	241
Monroe Randolph Saunders, Sr.	243

Willard E. Saunders	245
Alexander Robinson Schooler	246
David Schultz	248
Phillip Lee Scott	249
Lena Sears	250
Geneva Shelton	211
Samuel McDowell Shelton	252
Winfield Amos Showell	254
Alfred Singleton	256
Francis L. Smith	257
Helen Smith	258
Karl Franklin Smith	259
Willie Mae Ford Smith	261
Frank S. Solomon	263
Hebert Joseph Spencer	264
Cleveland H. Stokes	265
Marshall Taylor	267
Horace Temple	268
Robert Franklin Tobin	269
Lambert Roosevelt Tolbert	270
Joseph Morsel Turpin	271
Harrison Twyman	273
James Edison Tyson	274
Betty Showell Tyson	275
Norman Leonard Wagner	277
Charles Constantine Walsh	279
Christine Agatha Walsh	279
Charles William Watkins	280
Robert Allen Wauls	281

Joseph Weathers 282
Thomas John Weeks 283
George A. White 285
Melvina E. White 285
Frank W. Williams 287
Joseph David Williams 289
Roy Constantine Williams 290
McKinley Williams 291
Smallwood Edmond William 293
Quander Lear Wilson 297
Elzie William Young 299

Appendix: Representative Black Oneness Organizations 301
Appendix: Historical Events in the Black Oneness 305
Further Readings 307
Index of Names 313
Index of Organizations 319
Index of Terms 323

ACKNOWLEDGMENTS

To my wife, First Lady Augusta Showell, this work would not have been possible without your support and prayers. I want to thank Vanderlyn E. Hampton for her dedication and commitment to historical research, editing, and compiling this book. I would also like to thank my sons, Andre and Cornel, and the First Apostolic Faith Church Family.

FOREWORD

How appreciative we are to see the development and authorship of a publication that gives well-deserved recognition to Apostolic forerunners whose historical and spiritual legacies live on in us. Apostle Cornelius Showell is to be commended for his initiative in recognizing our great Pentecostal Apostolic heritage. While we know that God has the record, it is significant for our generation to preserve the memories of the contributions and sacrifices of our spiritual ancestors.

Those who have gone before us were model prayer warriors, workmen, and people whose sacrificial efforts resulted in many coming to faith in the Lord Jesus Christ. Many of the men and women honored in this book may not have graduated from the great colleges and universities or published articles in the major newspapers and magazines, but they were men and women of wisdom, who were directed by God's will and purpose to establish works that have stood the test of time. Showell reminds us of the rich spiritual history they have left to black Oneness Pentecostalism.

Bishop Robert C. Spellman, Ph.D., Historian
Church of Our Lord Jesus Christ of the Apostolic Faith, Inc
President, Church of Christ Bible Institute
Contender of the Faith, Editor

INTRODUCTION

The history of the black Apostolic movement is one that has often been neglected in the broader Pentecostal narrative. While Apostolic men and women have made significant contributions to Pentecostal theology, liturgy, hymnody, their story has never been entirely told. This work surveys the rise and development of Apostolic organizations from 1915 to the present and pays homage to the pioneers who were instrumental in growing Oneness Pentecostalism.

The movement began in Indianapolis, Indiana, in 1915, but its roots can be traced to the nineteenth-century Holiness movement. That movement's origins are rooted in the Methodist tradition, which taught piety, purity, and "entire sanctification" as a second work of grace. Several African American Holiness organizations including the United Holy Church of America, the Church of the Living God, the Fire-Baptized Holiness Church, and the Church of God in Christ would adopt Pentecostal spirituality. Some of these including the Church of God (Apostolic) and Triumph the Church and Kingdom of God in Christ would move into the Oneness/Apostolic tradition.

In 1900, a former Methodist minister, Charles Fox Parham instructed his Bethel Bible College students to examine the New Testament to determine the "biblical evidence" that one had received the baptism of the Holy Spirit. The students unanimously discovered speaking in tongues as the initial evidence of Spirit baptism. The most significant factor to emerge from Parham's Bible school was the correlation of Spirit baptism with glossolalia. However, Pentecostalism became a worldwide phenomenon under the leadership of Parham's former student. William J. Seymour, an African American, led the Azusa Street Revival in

1906 in Los Angeles, California. Black and white people across the United States and around the world visited Azusa. Several individuals who became prominent Apostolic leaders experience the outpouring of the Holy Spirit at the revival. From Azusa, over 200 Pentecostal organizations were birthed. Today, Pentecostalism is the fastest-growing segment in Christianity, with over 600 million adherents.

Oneness Pentecostalism had its direct beginnings at the 1913 Worldwide Camp meeting in Arroyo Seco, California. Canadian Pentecostal leader, Robert A. McAlister, preached a sermon on water baptism in which he noted that the early church in Acts administered the rite "in the name of Jesus" rather than the Trinitarian formula. His message was supported by a revelation to John Scheppe, who after a night of prayer confirmed the revelation of Jesus' name to the entire camp. This episode ignited the restoration of the New Testament teaching regarding baptism in Jesus' name and eventually led to the formulation of the doctrine of the Oneness of God.

Within a short time, the Oneness revival spread under two early Pentecostal leaders, Frank Ewart and Glen A. Cook. In 1915, Cook introduced the doctrine to Garfield T. Haywood, who would become an influential leader within the movement. The revival quickly spread among African Americans in Indianapolis, Indiana, and throughout the Midwest, South, Southwest, and East. In addition, the migration of blacks to urban cities such as New York, Chicago, Baltimore, Detroit, Washington, DC, and Philadelphia helped fuel the growth of the Apostolic movement. By 1920, six Apostolic organizations and hundreds of churches were founded. One hundred years after its beginning, the Oneness Pentecostals boast over 24 million people throughout America, the Caribbean, Africa, and Europe.

This work attempts to honor the men and women within the African Diaspora, especially in the United States, who have made significant contributions to this tradition and have been instrumental in spurring its growth.

In **Part I (Organizations and Fellowships)** we present the chronological unfolding of significant Apostolic organizations. Denominations included in this work range from small, loosely organized bodies with a few hundred members, to large bodies that number over a million members.

The biographical entries in **Part II (Pioneers and Leaders)** recount the lives and legacies of men and women of African descent who left an inedible mark on the movement. These include denominational founders, pastors of important congregations, educators, hymnists, civic leaders, and community activists.

This work is intended to be a resource for laypeople, scholars, researchers, and historians who are interested in this important movement within the African American Christian tradition. Yet, given the largely oral orientation within the movement, a major challenge in recounting this history has been the limited availability of institutional or biographical documentation from some bodies. Still these essays provide a starting point for those who wish to know more about this important segment of American Pentecostalism.

Part I:
Organizations and Fellowships

Pentecostal Assemblies of the World - 1915

The oldest and parent of most Black Apostolic/Oneness Pentecostal organizations. Pentecostal Assemblies of the World (PAW) began as an obscure fellowship shortly after the 1906 Azusa Street Revival. The first general assembly of the embryonic body was held in October 1907 in Los Angeles. At the time, the loose fellowship of Pentecostal congregations was neither black nor Oneness. One year later, the organization convened again in Los Angeles; that year, "Sister" Hopkins was elected temporary chairperson, and J. J. Frazee, who worked with Florence Crawford at the Apostolic Faith Mission in Portland, Oregon, was appointed Secretary. Hopkins held the office of chairperson until 1912 when Frazee was elected General Superintendent. After his election, PAW moved its base to Portland, Oregon.

Garfield T. Haywood, a recent African American Pentecostal convert and the pastor of the Apostolic Faith Assembly in Indianapolis, Indiana, obtained his credentials in 1911. His congregation later renamed Christ Temple, grew to become one of the largest interracial congregations in the city, and hosted annual conferences from 1913 to 1916. By 1915, the "new issue" concerning baptism in Jesus' name and the Oneness of God arose. Haywood had been skeptical about the new doctrine when early Oneness leader Glenn A. Cook first approached him. Nevertheless, he adopted the teaching, and in 1915 PAW became a Oneness organization. The new issue quickly spread throughout the Pentecostal movement, and many Assemblies of God (AOG) leaders embraced Oneness, thus fracturing the newly formed body into two factions, Trinitarian and Oneness. A General Council was held in October 1916 in St. Louis, Missouri, to settle the matter. The council issued a statement of faith that upheld Trinitarian beliefs, hence forcing out Oneness adherents. Former members of the AOG formed the General Assembly of the Apostolic Assemblies (GAAA) in 1917.

GAAA merged with PAW in 1918. At its first general meeting, Frazee was elected General Superintendent and Chairperson, D. C. O. Opperman was chosen as Secretary, and Howard Goss as treasurer. Haywood, Floyd I. Douglas, Robert C. Lawson, and A. R. Schooler were the only four blacks elected among the twenty-one field superintendents selected. In 1919, E. W. Doak replaced Frazee as chairman, and Haywood was appointed General Secretary. That year, PAW permanently moved its headquarters to Indianapolis and formally incorporated it in Indiana.

The move altered the racial complexion from predominantly white to where blacks represented the majority of its membership. Notable black leaders included Joseph M. Turpin, Oddous Barber, Dunlap Chenault, George Cooke, Samuel N. Hancock, Susan Lightford, J. C. Pratt, C. R. Wilkerson, and Herbert Davis. In 1919, Lawson, who served on the board of elders, resigned over the issues of divorce and remarriage. Later, he founded the Church of Christ of the Apostolic Faith, which he later renamed the Church of Our Lord Jesus Christ of the Apostolic Faith; his body became one of the most influential black Oneness bodies in the nation.

Racial strife soon arose among some white members as blacks moved into positions of authority. By the 1920s, white members insisted that meetings primarily held in northern cities be relocated to the South. In 1922, white ministers held separate meetings because of complaints about the economic burden of meeting in the North. In addition, some southern ministers feared backlash in the "Jim Crow" south because a "black man's name appeared on their credentials. In response, in 1923, the organization adopted "Resolution No. 4," calling for white credentials to be signed by white presbyters and black credentials to be signed by black presbyters. In addition, recommendations called for establishing an all-black Eastern Division and an all-white Southern Division. The General Board rejected both suggestions, the racial split was unavoidable, and most white members left the organization.

A year after the split, remaining ministers adopted an episcopal governmental structure and elected Haywood presiding bishop, along with an interracial board of two white men—G. B. Rowe and A. F. Varnell, and three black men, Haywood, A. R. Schooler, and Joseph M. Turpin. Haywood led the predominately black organization from 1925 to 1931. During his tenure, the National Sunday School Association was established, and the Foreign Mission Department was reorganized under the direction of Hilda Reeder. By 1930, PAW had over 2,000 churches throughout the United States, Africa, the Caribbean, Asia, India, and Palestine.

Haywood's sudden and untimely death in 1931 left a void in the leadership since no successor had been named. That September, white Apostolic Churches of Jesus Christ leaders proposed a merger with PAW, recommending two significant propositions. First, the organization would be renamed the Pentecostal Assemblies of Jesus Christ, and second, the episcopal governmental system would be replaced. Most leaders rejected the merger. However, a few prominent black leaders such as

Hancock, Turpin, Karl F. Smith, Austin A. Layne, and John S. Holly left and joined the newly formed Pentecostal Assemblies of Jesus Christ (PAJC). The body reorganized and elected Samuel J. Grimes as the second presiding bishop in 1932. Before his election, he served as a missionary in Liberia, West Africa, and the Christian Outlook magazine editor. In 1937, several black leaders who joined PAJC in 1931 returned after racial schism split their organization.

PAW began the 1950s with approximately 600 churches. The organizations' growth remained steady, however, in 1952, Hancock challenged Grimes' position as presiding bishop but was defeated in a run-off election held at the First Apostolic Faith Church in Baltimore, Maryland. In 1957, Hancock left and organized the Pentecostal Churches of the Apostolic Faith with David Collins, Heardie Leaston, and Willie Lee.

The organization celebrated its 50th Jubilee anniversary in 1965 in Indianapolis. At the time, it had approximately 550 churches and 450,000 members. Between 1919 and 1960, at least twelve separate major Oneness bodies were founded (directly or indirectly) out of PAW. Grimes presided for thirty-three years and oversaw the group after the death of Haywood, the failed merger with PAJC, and the split with Hancock. The National Pentecostal Young People's Union, the Women's Federation, and Aenon Bible College were organized during his leadership.

Ross P. Paddock, a white pastor from Kalamazoo, Michigan, served as Grimes' assistant presiding bishop and was elected the presider after Grimes' death in 1967. Paddock was elected to two full terms and served until 1974. Francis L. Smith of Akron, Ohio, succeeded Paddock as the fourth presiding bishop. He held that office for six years and was followed by Lawrence E. Brisbin, a white pastor from Grand Rapids, Michigan, who served from 1980 to 1986. James A. Johnson became the fifth presiding prelate, leading the organization until 1992 and was followed by Paul A. Bowers, who served until 1998. During the administrations of Johnson and Bowers, membership reached 1.5 million. Finally, Norman L. Wagner was elected in 1998, at the time, the youngest presider in history. Wagner served until 2004, when Horace E. Smith, a practicing physician, and pastor of the historic Apostolic Faith Church in Chicago, Illinois, was elected presiding bishop. In 2010, Smith was succeeded by Charles H. Ellis III, who served eight years.

PAW allows the ordination of women pastors, yet until the late 1990s, they were restricted from leadership positions such as district elder, diocesan bishop, and bishop. In 1995, Aletha J. Cushinberry was the first woman appointed district elder. She was elevated to the office of Suffragan Bishop in 2010 and, in 2015, was the first woman assigned to the office of honorary bishop. Currently, PAW has three women bishops. Mona Reide is a diocesan over the Sierra Leone District Council (West Africa), Gwendolyn G. Weeks serves as diocesan bishop over the South Africa District Council, and Ann Story Pratt holds the office of Suffragan bishop Emeritus of the state of Ohio.

Theodore L. Brooks, the son of apostolic pioneer George H. Brooks, is the current presider. Mark C. Tolbert serves as the 1st Assistant presiding bishop, and Michael Hannah is the 2nd Assistant Presiding Bishop. Today the organization has over 2 million members in more than 4,000 congregations around the globe.

Further Readings

Golder, Morris E. *The History of the Pentecostal Assemblies of the World.* Indianapolis: n.p., 1973.

Minute Book and Ministerial Record of the Pentecostal Assemblies of the World (Indianapolis: Pentecostal Assemblies of the World, 1918-1919).

Tyson, J. Laverne. *A Definitive History of the Pentecostal Assemblies of the World: A Narrative & Pictorial Study in 7 Volumes:* Volume 1, 1914–1930, Indianapolis: Tyson, 1998.

Church of God (Apostolic)

One of the earliest black apostolic bodies in America was initially known as the Christian Faith Band. The holiness church was founded in 1897 by a former slave, Thomas J. Cox. He incorporated his organization in 1901, establishing churches in Kentucky, Mississippi, Tennessee, and Arkansas. In 1915, Robert C. Lawson carried the apostolic message to parts of the south and southwest. He traveled to Kentucky and introduced the teaching to Cox, who embraced the doctrine.

Following his baptism, the organization held a special counsel at the General Assembly, and the Board of Elders moved to rename the organization to a more "scriptural name." The council recommended and voted to change the name to the Church of God, Apostolic (COGA) and was incorporated in 1919 in Paris, Kentucky. One of the first black apostolic organizations to embrace black liberation theology. In the section "The Black Man," the Doctrine and Disciplines rejects racial inferiority and asserts, "The word Negro was not given by the Lord. God called him Ethiopia.

Under Cox's leadership, COGA expanded into Ohio, West Virginia, North Carolina, Oklahoma, Florida, and Georgia. The organization reached its height in 1938 when it had more than 30,000 members and forty-nine congregations. Cox led the organization for forty years until poor health forced him to relinquish leadership. In 1943 Cox was succeeded by M. Gravely and Eli N. Neal as co-presiding bishops. The headquarters moved to Beckley, West Virginia. Two years later, Gravely was disfellowshipped.

After Gravely's departure, Neal assumed the position of presiding bishop. Within a short time of his coming into office, his authoritarian style alienated several ministers. Five elders—J. W. Audrey, James C. Richardson, Jerome Jenkins, W. R. Bryant, and J. M. Williams, who in 1940, left to form the Apostle Church of Christ in God in Winston-Salem, NC. In 1963, George Wiley, who had founded a congregation seven years earlier in Yonkers, New York, pulled out to establish Mt. Hebron Apostolic Temple of Our Lord Jesus Christ.

In 1964 Neal was succeeded by Love Odom, who served from 1964 to 1966. David E. Smith was elected presiding bishop after Odom. Smith, a gifted administrator, stabilized the finance of the national church. Unfortunately, the organization experienced another split under his leadership. In 1969, Johnnie Draft and Wallace Snow left to establish the Apostolic Church of Christ (Pentecostal). Reuben K. Hash replaced Smith after his death in 1975, and the church moved its headquarters from Beckley, West Virginia, to Saints Peter's Church in Winston-Salem, North Carolina. COGA membership declined from 30,000 to 15,000 members after several splits and schisms. The current presider of the body, Cecil O. Reid, oversees eighteen congregations in West Virginia, North Carolina, Georgia, Florida, Lima, Peru, and the continent of Africa.

Further Readings
Burton, Michael C. *Deep Roots: The African/Black Contribution to Christianity*, Bloomington, IN: IUniverse Inc, 2008.

Discipline and Manuel of Church of God Apostolic. Winston-Salem, NC: Church of God (Apostolic), n.p., n.d.

Apostolic Faith Mission Church of God

Frank W. Williams was one of the first African Americans to receive the baptism of the Holy Spirit at the Bonnie Brae Street prayer meeting, where William J. Seymour held his initial meetings before the Azusa Street Revival. After he received the baptism of the Holy Spirit, Williams took the Pentecostal message to Mississippi.

He later relocated to Mobile, Alabama, where he held a successful revival in which the entire congregation of the Primitive Baptist Church was converted. The church gave him their building, and Williams named the church the Apostolic Faith Mission because of his association with Seymour. Williams soon traveled throughout the South, establishing Pentecostal churches in Alabama, Florida, and Georgia. His Birmingham congregation, Saints Tabernacle, became the headquarters for the organization.

When the message of Jesus' Name baptism reached the South by 1915, Williams embraced the doctrine, incorporated his organization, and renamed it the Apostolic Faith Mission Church of God (AFMCG). His acceptance of baptism in Jesus' name caused him to split with his mentor Seymour. Williams led AFMCG for twenty-six years until his death in 1932. The Board of Elders took over the organization's leadership until 1963 when Houston Ward was elected presiding bishop. As presiding bishop, Ward instituted the ordination of women into ministry, the National Sunday School Department, the Young People's Christian Association, and the denomination increased from 2,600 to 15,400 during his leadership.

Donice Brown, the current presiding bishop, assumed leadership after Ward's death in 1993. By 2005, there were 10,730 members in eighteen churches, most of which were in

Alabama. By 2009, membership declined to 6,880 members in sixteen congregations. The body emphasizes divine healing, allows the ordination of women, and practices foot washing. It is led by a presiding bishop and cabinet of executive officers composed of bishops, overseers, and a general secretary. Apostolic Faith Mission Church of God remains a small regional organization located primarily in Alabama and Florida.

Further Reading
Tucker, Anjulet. "Apostolic Faith Mission Church of God." In *African American Religious Cultures*, edited by Stephen C. Finley and Torin Alexander, 88–90. Santa Barbara, CA: ABC-CLIO, 2009.

Apostolic Overcoming Holy Church of God - 1916

William Thomas Phillips founded the Ethiopian Overcoming Holy Church of God in Mobile, Alabama. The term "Ethiopian" denoted Phillips's emphasis on a religious movement promoting racial pride and black empowerment. He converted to Holiness and received the baptism of the Holy Spirit under the ministry of Frank W. Williams in 1913. Soon he began traveling throughout the South preaching as an evangelist.

In 1916, he embraced the revelation of baptism in the name of Jesus and formed the Ethiopian Overcoming Holy Church of God. Founded in the deep South at the height of racial segregation, the church embraced Marcus Garvey's Universal Negro Improvement Association and endorsed an early "black theology." Realizing that God's message was for all people and not one race, Phillips decided to rename the organization to reflect the inclusion of all races. In 1941, the body was incorporated in Alabama as the Apostolic Overcoming Holy Church of God (AOHC).

Phillips attempted to merge his organization with PAW and Glorious Church of God in Christ (GCOGIC) on two separate occasions. In 1934, Phillips attended PAW's general convention and addressed the delegation, but a merger never materialized. In 1940, after the death of Lulu Phillips, one of the founding members of GCOGIC, Phillips attended the annual meeting along with his Board of Bishops. He proposed that Glorious Church and his organization join fellowships yet remain autonomous bodies. Some GCOGIC leaders viewed his proposal with suspicion, believing he intended to take over the group. Unable to convince some leaders, Phillips focused attention on his growing organization, which had over 200 churches. By 1956, AOHC reported over 300 churches and a membership of 75,000 throughout the United States, Africa, West Indies, and India.

Phillips led AOHC for fifty-seven years. Jasper Roby succeeded him as presiding bishop and moved the organizational headquarters from Mobile to his home church AOHC Cathedral in Birmingham, Alabama. He also established the AOH Theological Seminary and School of Academic Studies. When Roby became ill and unable to serve as presider bishop in 2000, George W. Ayers was voted by the National Executive Board to serve as acting president. After a two-year legal battle, a fraction of AOHC leaders disagreed with his appointment. Finally, the Alabama Supreme Court named Ayers the rightful leader. Ayers became the presiding bishop in June 2000 after the death of Roby. John H. Matthews of Dayton, Ohio, succeeded Ayers as the presiding bishop in 2015. The current presider is Lawrence Williams from Tulsa, Oklahoma.

AOHC practices the ordination of women, divine healing, and foot washing and teaches the Wesleyan doctrine of three works of grace rather than the Finished Work doctrine many other Oneness/Apostolic organizations hold. The organization has an episcopal polity, though each church manages its affairs. Local churches are united under districts which overseers and diocesan bishops govern. A General Assembly, where all churches send representatives, convenes annually and is led by the presiding bishop. AOHC has 130 congregations throughout Maryland, Pennsylvania, New York, West Virginia, Alabama, Georgia, Tennessee, Arkansas, and Kentucky.

Further Reading

Arrington, Juanita Roby. *A Brief History of the Apostolic Overcoming Holy Church of God, Inc., and Its Founder: Including "What We Believe."* Birmingham, AL: Forniss, 1984.

Golder, Morris E. *The History of the Pentecostal Assemblies of the World.* Indianapolis: n.p., 1973, 116.

Payne, Leonard M. Jr. My People Yesterday, Today and Forever: A History of the Glorious Church of God in Christ. n.i.: Xlibris, 2008, 86.

Emmanuel Tabernacle Baptist Church of the Apostolic Faith

The first predominately black apostolic organization established in the Midwest was founded by Martin Rawleigh Gregory, a former Baptist minister. He moved to Columbus, Ohio, in 1914 and encountered the apostolic message under the influence of the preaching of Robert C. Lawson. Gregory's acceptance of Oneness Pentecostalism caused him to break with the Baptist church. Baptist ministers Lela Grant and Bessie Dockett also joined him and were ordained bishops sometime after; thus, ETBC was the first black apostolic body to ordain women bishops.

The church expanded its initial growth from Ohio into West Virginia, Virginia, and North Carolina. In 1922, Gregory encountered Mother Lulu Phillips, one of the founding leaders of the Glorious Church of God in Christ. She invited him to speak at her church in Huntington, West Virginia concerning baptism in Jesus' name and the Oneness of God. Phillips and fifty congregation members were baptized after hearing Gregory's teaching. Following her baptism, her organization adopted the Apostolic doctrine.

Gregory died in 1960 in West Virginia. Some of the bishops who succeeded him included O. J. Gentry; he served until he died in 1976. Thomas Carey did one year after Gentry. In 1978, H. C. Clark was appointed presiding bishop, becoming the first woman to serve in that position. She led the organization for twenty-eight years until her death in 2006. Clark was succeeded by F. C. Dampier, who resigned in 2013. The current presiding bishop is Edward M. Mitchell. The organization has approximately 30 churches located in Ohio, Florida, Maryland, West Virginia, Virginia, and North Carolina.

Church of Our Lord Jesus Christ of the Apostolic Faith - 1919

One of the largest Apostolic organizations in the United States was established in 1919 by Robert C. Lawson. Sometime in 1918, Lawson disagreed with G. T. Haywood, his "spiritual father" stance on divorce and remarriage. Unable to address his concerns at the 1919 PAW convention, he handed E. W. Doak who served as Chairmen his resignation. In July of that same year, he traveled to Harlem, New York City, and, beginning with a series of prayer meetings and street preaching services, founded Refuge Church of Christ of the Apostolic Faith.

While pastoring his work in Harlem, Lawson also pastored Apostolic Faith Assembly later named Church of Christ of the Apostolic Faith in Columbus, Ohio. He used his base church in Columbus to establish "Church of Christ" congregations in Philadelphia, Pennsylvania, San Antonio, Texas, and St. Louis, Missouri. He sent ministers to pastor churches and establish congregations throughout the East and Midwest. These ministers included Sherrod C. Johnson of Pennsylvania, Hebert J. Spencer of Ohio, Leroy J. Clifford of Connecticut, and Smallwood E. Williams who pastored Bible Way Church in Washington, DC.

Refuge Church quickly grew, and, with this growth, Lawson moved his headquarters from Columbus to Harlem in 1920. Later, he founded the Church of Christ Bible Institute as the theological training center for the organization in 1928. Under the administration of James I. Clark, Sr., the institute received full accreditation in 1950. He also established the Robert C. Lawson Institute in Southern Pines, North Carolina, which provided private elementary and secondary education to inner-city children. His organization was incorporated under the name Church of Our Lord Jesus Christ of the Apostolic Faith (COOLJC) in 1931.

By 1935, the organization had eighty churches throughout the United States, Virgin Islands, and Panama. Twenties years later, there were over 50,000 members and 175 churches worldwide, including Trinidad, Jamaica, and Africa. Several new auxiliaries and departments were created within the growing organization, including the International Women's Council, founded by Mother Delphia Perry in 1951. The official publications include a periodical, The Contender for the Faith, an annual magazine, an International Minute Book, which records activities of international auxiliaries and departments.

COOLJC experienced tremendous growth but also underwent several splits between 1933 and 1957. Sherrod C. Johnson, the state bishop of North Carolina and Pennsylvania, initiated the first major schism within the organization. Citing what he considered the organization's liberal dress code for women and Lawson's ecumenicism. Johnson organized the Church of the Lord Jesus Christ in 1933. With this split, Lawson lost churches in North Carolina and Pennsylvania. That same year, Henry C. Brooks, a charter member left and established Way of the Cross Church of Christ in Washington DC.

In 1938, another break took place when J. P. Shields founded Zion Gospel Assembly Churches in the Jamaica area of Queens, New York. Within a few years, Joseph D. Williams departed to form the Progressive Church of Our Lord Jesus Christ in Columbia, South Carolina, in 1944. The most significant split occurred in 1957, when Smallwood E. Williams, then-executive secretary, who pastored the second largest church in COOLJC, separated along with seventy churches and established Bible Way Church of Our Lord Jesus Christ World Wide. Several years later, John W. Pernell of Richmond, Virginia, organized Refuge Temple Assembly of Yahweh in 1970, and Lymus Johnson, who served as the National Evangelist, founded Evangelistic Churches of Christ.

COOLJC grew to become the third-largest Apostolic organization in the United States despite the numerous splits and schisms. At Lawson's death in 1961, 111 ministers were serving over 125 churches with 75,000 members. After Lawson, Hebert J. Spencer, William L. Bonner, and Maurice H. Hutner formed the Board of Apostles. Spencer was elected presiding bishop but retired in 1972 due to illness.

Bonner was elevated to the office of the presiding Apostle in 1973. Under his administration, the organization grew from 155 churches to over 500 congregations throughout the United States, Africa, the United Kingdom, Canada, Mexico, and India. He also founded the W. L. Bonner College in 1995 in Columbia, South Carolina. In 1989, Bonner was appointed Chief Apostle, however, he vacated the position of presiding bishop to Gentle Groover in 1995 but remained the Chief Apostle until his death at age ninety-three in 2015.

Groover served as presider until 2001. James I. Clark Jr. followed him from 2001 until 2007, Matthew Norwood served from 2007 until 2012, and Robert Sanders was presiding bishop from 2013 until 2016. Clark, the current presider, was again elected in 2016. Under his leadership, COOLJC launched the Social Justice, Economic and Racial Equality Commission to fight racism and poverty. COOLJC has spread to every state in the United States as well as many foreign countries in Canada, Liberia, West Africa, the United Kingdom, and Germany. Notably, over twenty black Apostolic bodies were birthed from the organization.

Further Reading

Spellman, Robert C., and Mable L. Thomas. *The Life, Legend, and Legacy of Bishop R.C. Lawson.* n.d: n.p, 1983.

Stewart, Alexander C, and Sherry S. DuPree. *The Silent Spokesman: Bishop Robert Clarence Lawson, Founder of the Church of Our Lord Jesus Christ of the Apostolic Faith, Inc.*, New York City. Gainesville, Fla: Displays for Schools, 1994.

Glorious Church of God in Christ – 1921

Mother Lulu Phillips and Cleveland H. Stokes co-founded the organization with former members of the Triumph the Church and Kingdom of God in Christ. Phillips moved to Huntington, West Virginia, and evangelized that city, establishing several churches under the Triumph Church Kingdom of God in Christ. In 1921, after the death of Elias D. Smith, the founder of Triumph Church, members called a meeting in Charlestown to restructure the church. From this meeting, Stokes adopted the name "Glorious Church of God in Christ," and Albart Simon was appointed the first presiding elder in 1922. That same year, Martin R. Gregory introduced Phillips to Oneness Pentecostalism, and the organization embraced the doctrine not too long after. Sidney Coy Bass assumed leadership after Simon's death in 1928.

Phillips was elected General Mother and served until she died in 1939. Besides Phillips, several women, including Mamie Whitehurst, Julia Robinson, and Beulah Reed were instrumental in the growth of GCOGIC. The organization appointed Bass the first General Bishop in 1944 and the body organized its first Sunday school department and newspaper, "The Gospel Banner News."

However, a major schism occurred when Bass went against church polity and married a divorced woman. His actions led to the withdrawal of twenty-five churches and the formation of The Original Glorious Church of God in Christ, under the leadership of W.O. Howard in 1955. Bass served as presider for thirty-eight years. Wesley Allen Wilson became the second General Presiding Bishop after the death of Bass in 1977. Wilson served one year and was subsequently elevated to the position of Honorary General Bishop in 1978.

Perry Lindsay Sr., the brother-in-law of Bass, succeeded Wilson in 1978. Lindsay's administration skills brought a new structure to the body after several years of schisms, power struggles, and a decline in membership. He presided over the organization for thirty-five years until he died in 2014. Azel C. Colston, Jr. is the current General Bishop. The organization is governed by a general board of Elders and has over two thousand members with sixteen churches in New York, New Jersey, Virginia, and West Virginia.

Further Reading
Payne, Leonard M. Jr. *My People Yesterday, Today and Forever: A History of the Glorious Church of God in Christ*. n.i.: Xlibris, 2008.

The Churches of God and True Holiness – 1927

Bishop John Wesley Garlington, Sr., established this group in Buffalo, New York. He expanded his base and added churches in New York, Virginia, North Carolina, Ohio, Florida, Delaware, and South Carolina. Garlington led the organization until his death in 1943, when Thomas Benton of Norfolk, Virginia, became the presiding bishop.

Frank Jackson of Winter Haven, Florida, assumed the post of presiding bishop after Benton's death in 1958. Jackson served until 1961; during his tenure, several doctrinal issues arose that caused a fracture when Joseph Peeler of Buffalo was appointed presider. Following Peeler's death three years later, John Kennon undertook the office until he relinquished his position to John W. Garlington, Jr., son of the founder.

Garlington, Jr. stepped down in 1975 and moved his family to Portland, Oregon, to assume the pastorate of a multi-cultural non-denominational congregation. Due to a fire at the headquarters church in Buffalo, the 47th Holy Convocation in 1974 was held in Rochester, New York, where the host pastor was Paul Garlington. Frank Jackson became the new presiding bishop on the departure of Garlington in 1975, and the national headquarters was relocated to the church in Cleveland, Ohio. Albert E. Dixon, Sr., who served as the national evangelist, succeeded Jackson in 1978.

He led the body for over thirty years and was followed by James Brant Jr. Under his leadership, the organization purchased a church in Buffalo, New York, which was its initial birthplace. Raymond Faison Jr., who served as 2nd Vice President, was elected as the presiding prelate in 2017 after the sudden death of

Brant in 2016. Today, the body has fourteen churches in Florida, Maryland, New York, North Carolina, Ohio, South Carolina, Virginia, and one congregation in Canada.

Way of the Cross Church of Christ - 1933

Bishop Henry Chauncey Brooks formed one of the East Coast's historic organizations. He established the Way of the Cross Church of Christ congregation in 1927 in Washington, DC. At the time, Way of the Cross was an independent church, not affiliated with any organization. Brooks traveled to Baltimore, Maryland, hoping to join Pentecostal Assemblies of the World, but the organization rejected his request. A few months later, James T. Morris, the founder of Highway Christian Church, introduced Brooks to Bishop Robert C. Lawson. In 1928, the church became a charted church under the Church of Christ of the Apostolic Faith.

Five years later, in 1933, Way of the Cross Church of Christ (WOTCC) became independent, and Brooks was consecrated to the office of bishop. He expanded his base in Washington DC by founding congregations in Maryland, Virginia, North Carolina, Pennsylvania, New York, and New Jersey. Brooks served as the presiding bishop for thirty-four years. Under his leadership, the organization grew to 5,000 members and thirty churches.

In 1967 Brooks' brother-in-law, John Luke Brooks succeeded him as the presiding bishop. During his administration, seven churches were added in Ghana and West Africa. However, two prominent pastors, Joseph Weathers and Joseph H. Adams split during his tenure. In 1969, Weathers broke away to form a local church, Holy Temple Church of Christ, in Washington, DC. Years later, in 1974, Joseph H. Adams of Axton, Virginia, pulled out of the organization to organize United Way of the Cross Churches of Christ of the Apostolic Faith. Harry Clay Eggleston became the third presiding bishop in 1981 and served in that position until his death in 1985.

Upon taking on the role of the fourth presiding prelate, LeRoy Cannady initiated a new organizational structure into WOTCC with the development of an Executive Board of Bishops, General Board of Bishops, and Pastoral Council, Ministers, and Elders Council, and National Sunday School Department. Thirteen additional churches in the United States and missions in Ghana and Liberia were also added. Cannady relinquished his position in 2015, and Alphonzo D. Brooks, the late founder's son, became the fifth Presiding Bishop. Brooks established the Apostolic Christian College and the Sound of Pentecost Radio Broadcast. Earley Dillard of Martinsville, Virginia, serves as the presiding bishop and general overseer. The body consists of sixty-eight churches in twelve states; seventy-two in India; forty-seven in Liberia; thirty-five in Nigeria; and ten in Haiti.

Further Reading
Way of the Cross Church of Christ. *85th Church Anniversary and Founder's Celebration* Journal. Washington, DC: Way of the Cross Church of Christ, Inc., 2012.

Church of the Lord Jesus Christ of the Apostolic Faith

The organization was established by Bishop Sherrod C. Johnson when he separated from the parent organization, Church of Our Lord Jesus Christ of the Apostolic Faith. Johnson was introduced to the Apostolic message and baptized in the name of Jesus under the ministry of Henry Prentiss in Philadelphia, Pennsylvania. He was ordained and assigned the pastorate of the Philadelphia Church of Christ by Robert C. Lawson in 1920. Over the next ten years, Johnson built that church into the second-largest Pentecostal congregation in that city. Johnson split with Lawson over what he considered the organization's liberal dress code for women.

He expanded his base via his Sunday broadcasts on WOOK in Washington DC and WIBC in Philadelphia. Three years after the split with Lawson, there were churches in eighteen states and several foreign countries. An ardent and staunch supporter of the Oneness doctrine, Johnson openly challenged his critics to debate him on his popular radio broadcast, "The Whole Truth," which aired to over ninety stations throughout the United States, Haiti, Bahamas, Great Britain, and Portugal.

Church of the Lord Jesus Christ of the Apostolic (COTLJC) stressed head coverings for women, forbade them to straighten their hair, and required them to wear long dresses. They also insisted that men within the organization wear dark-colored suits and be clean-shaven. In addition, the observance of traditional holidays such as Christmas and Easter were prohibited.

While on an evangelistic tour in 1961 in Jamaica, British West Indies, Johnson died at age sixty-three. At his death, the organization had over 50,000 members in the United States, Canada, and the Caribbean. Samuel McDowell Shelton, the general secretary, was elected as bishop and overseer. Shortly after he took over, Randolph Goodwin pulled out and founded Holy Temple Church of the Lord Jesus Christ of the Apostolic Faith in 1961. During his tenure, Shelton traveled globally, meeting with world leaders such as King Hussein of Jordan, Emperor Haile Selassie of Ethiopia; Pope Paul VI at the Vatican in Rome; and Prime Minister Indira Gandhi of India. By 1980, under Shelton's direction, COTLJC grew to more than one hundred congregations in the United States, England, Africa, Jamaica, and the Bahamas. Another split occurred in 1984 when a young minister named Gino Jennings left and founded the First Church of Our Lord Jesus Christ.

Upon his death in 1991, a legal battle erupted among his adopted sons Elder Nehemiah Shelton, Prince Omega Y. L. Shelton, and Bishop Anthonee Patterson over succession and control over his assets. Omega Shelton claimed the legal right of succession. He was appointed general overseer in 1992 and is the current leader of congregations in the United States, the Caribbean, Europe, and West Africa. Shelton made several progressive changes in the organization including a liberal stance on dress codes for men and women.

Further Reading
Johnson, Sherrod C. *21 Burning Subjects: Who is This that Defies and Challenges the Whole Religious World on these Subjects.* Philadelphia, PA: Church of Our Lord Jesus Christ of the Apostolic Faith, 1962.

Zion Gospel Churches of the Apostolic Faith - 1938

Bishop Judge Pierce (J. P.) Shields established Zion Assembly Church in Jamaica, Queens, New York. He began his ministry in the Church of Our Lord Jesus Christ of the Apostolic Faith, organizing Refuge Church of Christ in 1927. Shields left the parent body, and his congregation in Queens became the headquarters. He renamed his organization Zion Gospel Church, Inc, and he assumed the position of general bishop.

In 1996 his son, Bishop Waddell P. "Del" Shields, a well-known community activist and radio broadcaster, took over the pastorate of Zion Gospel. Shields hosted the "Night Call" on WRVR. The program allowed listeners to engage with African American leaders, including James Baldwin, Rev. Ralph Abernathy, Muhammad Ali, H. Rap Brown, Roy Innis, Eldredge Cleaver, Stokely Carmichael, and Dick Gregory. Shield and his congregation were actively involved in social issues until his death in 2015. Unfortunately, there is no current data or records on this organization.

Highway Christian Church of Christ - 1941

Pentecostal Assemblies of the World minister James T. Morris organized Highway Church in 1927 in Washington, DC. In 1941, he was consecrated as a bishop by Joseph M. Turpin, and that same year, he launched his organization. Morris traveled extensively, establishing forty-three congregations throughout DC, Virginia, New York, North Carolina, and South Carolina. In 1955 Raymond F. Davis, who had served as National Secretary and Overseer of the State of South Carolina, resigned his tenure and birthed Highway Church of Christ Association, Incorporated.

Morris' nephew, Jesse V. Lomax, a former member of the Church of Our Lord Jesus Christ, succeeded him as presiding bishop in 1959. However, during Lomax's tenure, a schism occurred within the ranks of HCCC during his term. First, in 1976 James Frank Harris and Douglas Williams separated to establish the Redeemed Assembly of Jesus Christ, Apostolic. Then, when Lomax died in 2001, Samuel Redden replaced him. By 2002, the organization had approximately three thousand members and nineteen congregations in Washington DC, New York, Virginia, North Carolina, and South Carolina. Bishop Herman Ginwright, who served as National Secretary and is the pastor of the Headquarters Church in Washington, DC, is the current presiding prelate.

Apostle Church of Christ in God

Five elders co-founded the Apostle Church of Christ in God (ACCG) - J. W. Ardrey, James C. Richardson Sr, Jerome Jenkins, W. R. Bryant, and J. M. Williams. The group's origins can be traced to the Christian Faith Band founded by Thomas J. Cox in 1897. Cox embraced the Oneness doctrine in 1915 and incorporated his organization under the new name, Church of God Apostolic. Eli N. Neal assumed the role of acting presiding bishop. However, sometime later, some pastors and ministers expressed concerns over the authoritarian way Neal conducted the organization's affairs. Unable to resolve their differences, Ardrey, Richardson, Jenkins, Bryant, and Williams pulled out to establish the Apostle Church of Christ God in 1941.

Ardrey was elected the first presiding bishop, and several congregations were added in North Carolina, Virginia, South Carolina, Pennsylvania, and New York. In 1952, the organization elevated Richardson as the second bishop and he assisted Ardrey. One year after, Robert O. Doub, the overseer of Pennsylvania left to organize Shiloh Apostolic Temple after dissatisfaction with Ardrey's leadership.

In 1956, Richardson became the presiding bishop after Ardrey resigned. His tenure prompted growth within the ACCG. He started the Apostolic Gazette (later the Apostolic Journal) and established a program to assist ministers in pursuing education. However, several schisms slowed the organization's progress under Richardson's leadership. The most prominent division occurred in 1970 when Audrey, the former presider, left to find an independent congregation.

By 1980, membership had grown to 2,150 members in thirteen congregations served by five bishops and twenty-five ministers. Richardson presided for thirty-nine years. In 1995, after his death, his son, James C. Richardson Jr., assumed the position and is the current presiding prelate. Robert Conward serves as 1st Vice presider, and Harry J. Betts is the Vice presiding bishop. Richardson Jr. oversees Virginia, Washington, DC, and North Carolina congregations.

Further Reading
Richardson, James C. Jr. *With Water and Spirit: A History of Black Apostolic Denominations in the U.S.* Washington DC: Spirit, 1980.

Progressive Church of Our Lord Jesus Christ - 1944

The Progressive Church of Our Lord (PCOOLJC) Jesus Christ was established by Joseph D. Williams Sr., who founded Pilgrim Church of Christ in Cleveland, Ohio, under the affiliation of the Church of Our Lord Jesus Christ. He resigned from the pastorate with Bishop Robert C. Lawson's approval and relocated to Columbia, South Carolina. Williams established the first church of his newly formed organization in 1944 following the miraculous healing of Helen L. Washington, one of his charter members. The congregation moved into their new edifice one year later, which Lawson rededicated.

Between the 1940s and 1950s, Williams traveled throughout South Carolina to preach and establish churches, and because of his effort, congregations were established in Killian, Mullins, Denmark, Lugoff, and Florence. Unfortunately, in 1963 a major split occurred in the organization, and several of the leading ministers, deacons, and members who had worked with Williams for many years left the organization.

Before his death, he appointed a Board of Elders to provide leadership for the group after his passing. Elders Joel G. Washington, Edward Smith, Herman Jackson, Henry J. Breakfield, and Ernest Finkley were left to decide who would succeed in his position. Williams served for twenty-two years as a pastor and presiding bishop. The board jointly governed after his death in 1966, with Washington serving as Chairperson. After Jackson's resignation, each elder oversaw a district of local churches to maintain the unity of the organization. In 1973, the Board of Elders was consecrated to the office of bishop and subsequently as the Board of Bishops. Members of the board elected Bishop

Joel G. Washington from Columbia, South Carolina, as presiding bishop in 1973. Washington sent ministers out throughout the United States, and as a result, PCOOLJC added ten churches. During the 1970s and 1980s, congregations started in North Carolina, Georgia, and Florida.

The organization ratified a new church Constitution and appointed Edward Smith as assistant presiding bishop in 1983. He assumed the position of presiding bishop when Washington died in 1987. Smith established a National Unity Conference for the National Church, and in 1999 Progressive Church dedicated a 2.5 million dollar, 31,000-square-foot Headquarters Church Complex with a 1,000-seat sanctuary, a family life center, a gymnasium, and classrooms. Smith served as the presiding prelate from 1987 to 2020. The current presiding bishop, Theodore Jenkins, Sr., oversees twenty-three churches and missions in North and South Carolina, Florida, Georgia, New York, and Africa.

Church of God in Jesus Christ (Apostolic) - 1946

Randolph A. Carr, a native of Nevis, West Indies, established the Church of God in Jesus Christ Apostolic (COGICJA) in Baltimore, Maryland. His early ministry began in Pentecostal Assemblies of the World. However, he later joined the Trinitarian organization, Church of God in Christ. In 1934, Charles H. Mason, the founder, sent him to Baltimore to pastor a small church organized by Mother Emily Mayfield in her home.

In 1946, a dispute arose over the practice of baptism in Jesus' name. As a result, Carr left COGIC and renamed his local congregation, Rehoboth Church of God in Jesus Christ Apostolic, and organized Church of God in Jesus Christ Apostolic. Early leaders included Monroe R. Saunders of Baltimore, Maryland, Sr; Sydney A. Dunn of Birmingham, England; John S. Watson of Jamaica, West Indies; Elmer F. Akers, General Secretary; and Peter J. F. Bridges, Treasurer.

Congregations quickly spread along the East Coast of the United States and Great Britain. Under the leadership of Bridges, COGICJA expanded into Jamaica and later merged with Emmanuel Apostolic United Church of Christ, led by Jamaican apostolic leader Melvina E. White. The merger lasted only a few years, but Carr's organization had added several churches that remain today in Jamaica.

In 1965 Saunders, Dunn, and Watson disagreed with Carr regarding organizational polity. As a result, Saunders established the United Church of Jesus Christ (Apostolic). William S. Barnes presided over the organization after the death of Carr in 1970. He instituted an International Women's Council, International

Brotherhood, and appointed women as voting members of the Governing Board. By 2008, COGICJA reported more than 50 churches throughout the United States and Canada, Jamaica, Bermuda, and the West Indies.

William J. Faison Sr. followed Barnes and served until his death in 2017. Following him, Williams S. Barnes, Jr. briefly served from 2017 to 2018. The current presiding bishop is Harry R. Wilson Jr. COGICJA churches are located primarily in Maryland, Virginia, North and South Carolina, Delaware, Ohio. There are also congregations in Jamaica, St. Kitts, Nevis, and the US Virgin Islands.

Further Reading

Gerloff, Roswith I.H. *A Plea for British Black Theologies: The Black Church Movement in Britain in Its Transatlantic Cultural and Theological Interaction, with Special Reference to the Pentecostal Oneness (Apostolic) and Sabbatarian Movements. Part 1*. Frankfurt am Main: Peter Lang, 1992.

Original Glorious Church of God in Christ – 1955

The Glorious Church of God in Christ (OGCOGIC) was founded by Mother Lulu Phillips and Cleveland H. Stokes in 1921. Sydney C. Bass moved into the position of General Overseer after the death of Albart Simon, the first presiding elder, in 1928. The organization appointed Bass the first General Bishop in 1944, and he served as presider for thirty-eight years. However, a major schism occurred under his administration when he went against church polity and married a divorced woman. His actions led to the resignation of prominent leaders, Stokes, W. O. Howard, Quander L. Wilson, and Isaiah W. Hamiter, and the formation of the OGCOGIC in 1955.

The group took the name "Original" signifying its claim to its history and the retention of the founding charter. Howard, who held the original charter, was appointed presiding bishop and served in that office from 1955 to 1972. Under his leadership, the church added fifteen congregations; however, in 1960, Wilson, one of the founding members, left to start Greater Emmanuel Apostolic Tabernacle.

In 1972, Howard retired because of poor health and was succeeded by Hamiter from Columbus, Ohio. He expanded the organization's mission programs in Haiti, Jamaica, and India. Melvin M. Maughmer became the presiding bishop after the death of Hamiter in 1985. Maughmer had the distinction of officiating the ordination of the first two female bishops. In 2013, Dr. Julia M. Shaffer, pastor of God's House of Prayer and Deliverance Holiness Church of Cleveland, Ohio, and Rocine Jackson, pastor of the Original Glorious Church of God in Christ in Whitman, West Virginia, were consecrated to the office of bishop.

The current presiding bishop of Original Glorious Church is Bishop Charles M. Laster. In 2020, OGCOGIC began plans to build a multi-million dollar, 57,538-square-foot headquarters and multi-purpose facility in Cleveland, Ohio.

Further Reading

Payne, Leonard M. Jr. *My People Yesterday, Today and Forever: A History of the Glorious Church of God in Christ*. n.i.: Xlibris, 2008.

Highway Churches of Christ

Raymond F. Davis served as National Secretary in Highway Christian Church of Christ under the direction of Bishop James T. Morris. He resigned from HCCC along with Alfred Bell and Fred A. Page and launched Highway Church of Christ in Marion, South Carolina, in 1955. The board of Elders ordained him bishop over the new body in 1958. Davis established congregations throughout North and South Carolina and other churches in New Jersey, Maryland, New York, Pennsylvania, and Massachusetts during the 1960s and 1970s.

The organization experienced one major schism when in 1989, Robert Evans, who pastored Beth-El Temple in Baltimore, left and established Beth-El Churches of Christ, Inc. Following Evans departure, Highway added churches in North Carolina, Pennsylvania, New York, and South Carolina. Sometime later, Davis renamed his group Greater Highway Church of Christ, Incorporated. The current presiding bishop is Bishop Malachi Haines, appointed after Davis died in 2017. Haines governs churches in South Carolina and throughout the eastern region of the United States, Jamaica, and West Africa.

Pentecostal Churches of the Apostolic Faith - 1957

One of the twelve influential organizations to be birthed out of the Pentecostal Assemblies of the World was founded by Bishop Samuel N. Hancock with Bishops Willie Lee, Heardie Leaston, and Elder David Collins. Hancock, the pastor of Greater Bethlehem Temple, one of the largest apostolic churches in the United States during the 1920s, rose to prominence as an early leader of PAW. The newly formed group quickly added churches throughout the Midwest, South, and East. Hancock headed PCAF for six years.

Under the charismatic leader, the church had over 600 churches. After Hancock's death in 1963, Willie Lee, who served as pastor of Christ Temple in Indianapolis, Indiana, succeeded him. He held the position briefly from 1963 to 1964. For many years, Hancock taught that Jesus was only a son of God, not God himself. Lee also held the same beliefs. However, when PCAF leaders adopted the traditional apostolic doctrine, Lee started a separate group, Emmanuel Pentecostal Church of Our Lord Apostolic Faith.

Elzie W. Young, who pastored the Greater Bethlehem Temple in Cincinnati, Ohio, replaced Lee as presiding bishop. The organization had 25,000 members in the United States, Haiti, and Liberia during his tenure. The longest-serving presider, Young led PCAF for twenty-five years until his death at seventy-six in 1989.

D. Rayford Bell followed Young in 1990. He established the Midwest Apostolic Bible College and Samuel Barnes Christian Academy. From Lansing, Michigan, Alfred Singleton took over after Bell and served from 2000 until 2008. J. E. Moore served two terms as Presiding Bishop from 2008 to 2016. Bishop Lambert W.

Gates from Detroit, Michigan, serves as pastor of Mt. Zion Apostolic Church in Indianapolis, Indiana is the current presiding bishop. The PCAF headquarters is located in Louisville, Kentucky, and the official publication is Voice in the Wilderness. Today, PCAF has over 400 churches across the United States in Haiti and Liberia.

Bible Way Church of Our Lord Jesus Christ World Wide

The Bible Way Church of Our Lord Jesus Christ World Wide had its inception in September 1957. That year, Smallwood E. Williams convened a National Pentecostal Ministerial Conference to consider some "mal-administrative" practices out of line with New Testament collective leadership as practiced by the Apostles. As a result, Williams, who served as General Secretary of the Church of Our Lord Jesus Christ of the Apostolic Faith, withdrew from the parent body with seventy churches. At the National Pentecostal Ministerial Conference, Williams, John S. Beane, McKinley Williams, Winfield A. Showell, and Joseph Moore were consecrated to the office of bishop by PAW leader, John S. Holly.

Within five years after its formation, the organization had established a successful Missionary Department, Sunday School, Women's Council, and Youth Department. The Foreign Missions department included over 60 churches in the West Indies, seven churches in London, England, and several in Liberia, West Africa. As a result, Bible Way grew from seventy to 300 churches and 100,000 members ten years later.

Williams, the establishmentarian who founded the Bible Way Church in Washington DC in 1927, presided over Bible Way for thirty-four years. In 1991, the organization had approximately 300,000 members in 365 congregations in the United States, Great Britain, Jamaica, Trinidad and Tobago, Liberia, and Nigeria at the time of his death.

John S. Beane, one of the founding leaders, had been a member of COOLJC since the 1920s. He founded Bethesda Church of Christ in Petersburg, Virginia. Beane also served as State

Overseer and national treasurer. Within Bible Way, he served as the first treasurer, vice-bishop, and diocesan of the Virginia State Diocese until he died in 1973.

McKinley Williams was also affiliated with COOLJC. He organized Refuge Church of Christ in Philadelphia, Pennsylvania, and worked alongside Sherrod C. Johnson, the State Overseer of COOLJC in Pennsylvania. As one of the founding leaders of Bible Way, Williams served as vice-presiding bishop and Diocesan over Pennsylvania and Georgia for twenty-four years.

Winfield A. Showell was the only founding leader, not a "spiritual" son of Robert C. Lawson, and was not a former member of COOLJC. At the time, he was associated with Pentecostal Assemblies of the World. Showell served as pastor of First Apostolic Faith Church in Baltimore, Maryland. He succeeded Bishop Joseph M. Turpin, who founded the church and was one of the original five bishops of PAW. In Bible Way, Showell served as a vice-presiding bishop, Diocesan over the New Jersey Diocese, Central Maryland and Delaware Diocese, Ohio, Jamaica, and West Indies Diocese for thirty years.

Joseph Moore served as assistant pastor at Refuge Church of Christ for ten years in Brooklyn, New York. He established the Bibleway Church of Our Lord Jesus Christ in Brooklyn in 1943. Moore served the Diocesan of New York, Connecticut, and Massachusetts until his death in 1966.

Before his death, Williams established an order of succession which stated that his successor, Lawrence G. Campbell, and Huie L. Rogers would each serve three-year terms. Campbell founded Bible Way Church of Our Lord Jesus Christ in Danville, Virginia, and was the first to succeed Williams as presiding bishop, serving from

1991 to 1994. Rodgers pastored the Bible Way Church in Brooklyn, New York. He served as presiding bishop from 1994 to 1997. In 1998, at the end of Rogers's term, Campbell was nominated to head Bible Way, receiving 11 of 18 votes from the Board of Bishops and 28 of 39 votes from the Joint Board of Bishops. Unable to reach a consensus in leadership, a split occurred within the organization. That same year, Campbell became the Chief Apostle presiding bishop of the International Bible Way Church of Jesus Christ (IBW). He served from 1998 to 2006. Rogers served as the presiding bishop of Bible Way Church of Our Lord Jesus Christ World Wide from 1998 to 2019. He remains the Chief Apostle of the parent body. His son, Michael J. Rogers, is the current presider.

In 2006, Cornelius Showell, the son of Bishop Winfield A. Showell, was elected presiding bishop and Chief Apostle of IBW. Showell advocated for the ordination of women to the office of Elder, and he established the Leadership Development Institute and served from 2006 to 2014. Floyd E. Nelson Sr. was appointed presiding bishop and Chief Apostle in 2014. Under his leadership, Bonnie Hunter became the first woman to be ordained to the office of bishop. The current presiding prelate is Apostle Willie E. Rookard of Inman, South Carolina. He assumed the position after the death of Nelson in 2019. IBW has over 350 churches in the United States and 250 congregations throughout Europe, Asia, Africa, South America, and the Caribbean.

Bible Way Pentecostal Apostolic Church - 1960

Bishop Curtis P. Jones, a pastor in the Church of God (Apostolic) in Winston-Salem, North Carolina, founded Bible Way Pentecostal Apostolic Church. In 1933, Eli N. Neal, COGA state overseer, sent Jones to Roanoke, Virginia, to establish a church. There he organized the Star of Bethlehem Apostolic Church. Jones resigned after five years in 1938 after several years of dissatisfaction with the leadership of Thomas J. Cox. He joined the Church of Our Lord Jesus Christ under Bishop Robert C. Lawson and became the pastor of St. Paul Apostolic Church in Henry County, Virginia.

In 1957, Smallwood E. Williams, who served as General Secretary in COOLJC, convened a meeting in Washington, DC, at the National Ministerial Conference where he and John S. Beane, McKinley Williams, Winfield A. Showell, and Joseph Moore were consecrated to the office of bishop in the newly formed Bible Way Church of Our Lord Jesus Christ. Jones attended the meeting as part of a delegation from Virginia but decided not to join Williams.

Instead, in 1960, he left COOLJC and formed Bible Way Pentecostal Apostolic Church. Bible Way Pentecostal began with two congregations in Virginia but later added two other churches. Jones led the organization until 1976. General Elder Edward Martin, who many believed would assume the position as presiding bishop, faced opposition and never was accepted as presider. Today, Joe H. Adkins is the current overseer and pastor of Bible Way Pentecostal Apostolic Church.

Greater Emmanuel Fellowship International

Greater Emmanuel Apostolic Faith Tabernacles was organized by Quander L. Wilson, a pastor and former General Secretary in the Glorious Church of God in Christ, from 1953 to 1955. Wilson was also one of the founding members of the Original Glorious Church of God in Christ. He left the group in 1960 and formed his organization with two congregations in Portsmouth and Burlington, Ohio. Greater Emmanuel birthed the ministries of many well-known pastors and ministers. But, perhaps, the best known is the famed pastor and preacher Thomas Dexter (T. D.) Jakes was a regional bishop until 1988, when he joined Sherman S. Watkins's organization Higher Ground Always Abounding Assemblies.

In 2000, because of failing health, Wilson called a "Special Call Meeting," he turned the organization's reins over to Edward E. Shouse Sr., the current presider. Shouse organized the "School without Walls," the institution achieved accreditation with the Apostolic University of Indianapolis, Indiana. He is a member of the World Fellowship of Pentecostal Churches, Apostolic World Christian Fellowship, and the National Evangelical Association. Greater Emmanuel headquarters remains in Portsmouth, Ohio, and congregations are in Ohio, West Virginia, Pennsylvania, New York, Missouri, Texas, Michigan, and Africa.

True Vine Pentecostal Churches of Jesus - 1961

Bishop Robert Leonard Hairston, a former leader of the Trinitarian group, the True Vine Pentecostal Holiness Churches, formed the True Vine Pentecostal Churches of Jesus. Hairston was the cofounder of True Vine Pentecostal Holiness Churches with William Monroe Johnson in 1946. He served as vice presiding for fifteen years. However, conflict arose between the two men during the 1960s over church polity and the divorce of Hairston. In 1961, Hairston adopted the apostolic teaching of baptism in Jesus' name, True Vine Pentecostal Holiness Churches, a Trinitarian group removed him from the office of the vice presider. He left the church and founded the True Vine Pentecostal Churches of Jesus.

By 1976, True Vine added new churches when Bishop Thomas C. Williams brought several congregations into the body and several independent churches affiliated with them. Sometime later, Williams was appointed senior bishop and remained the presiding bishop until his death in 1991. The organization has ten congregations and missions and approximately nine hundred members. True Vine headquarters is at Greater New Bethel Apostolic Church in Martinsville, Virginia. The church was pastored by the late Bishop Mark Price, who served as vice president of the organization.

Free Gospel Churches of the Apostles' Doctrine – 1962

Based in the Baltimore/Washington DC region, Free Gospel Churches of the Apostles' Doctrine was organized by Bishop Ralph E. Green. In 1962, he founded Free Gospel Deliverance Temple, which became one of the mega-churches in Prince George's County, Maryland. Free Gospel had three churches in Maryland, two in Virginia, and one congregation in North Carolina within a few years. In addition, Green founded the Open Bible Institute for Christian Apologetics as the theological training center for his organization. He also established a bookstore and published a monthly periodical outreach for prison ministries, From Prison to Praise.

The organization initially did not ordain women. However, Green changed his stance and, in 2004, appointed his wife, Dr. Shirley Green, senior pastor of Free Gospel Deliverance Temple. In 2011, four women were ordained as ministers of the gospel for the first time in the organization. By 2018, at the time of his death, Free Gospel had congregations throughout the District of Columbia, Maryland, North Carolina, Virginia, Africa, and the Philippines. Today, Green's daughter, Antoinette Green Snow serves as presiding pastor of Free Gospel Deliverance Temple.

Apostolic Inter-Organizational Fellowship Conference- 1963

Bishop Smallwood E. Williams, the founder of Bible Way Church of Our Lord Jesus Christ, envisioned a unified black Apostolic movement. So, in 1963, at Bible Way Church in Washington, DC, he brought together 100 Pentecostal leaders from various Apostolic organizations to address foreign missions, evangelism, Christian education, higher education, a ministerial conference, and a layman's council. From this conference, the Apostolic Inter-Organizational Fellowship Conference (AIFC) was born. Williams was elected chairman at the organizing meeting, John W. Pernell, the founder of Refuge Temple Assembly of Yahweh, was elected vice-chairman, and Pentecostal Assemblies of the World leader John S. Holly was Treasurer.

The AIFC met at the Greater Refuge Temple in New York City in 1971, and leaders representing PAW were David A. Shultz, Frank R. Bowdan, Freeman Thomas, and Frances L. Smith. Representatives from COOLJC included Hubert J. Spencer, presiding bishop, Lymus Johnson, Frank S. Solomon, and George Marshall. J. V. Lomax of Highway Christian Church of Christ, Joseph Weathers, founder of Holy Temple Church of Christ, and Monroe Saunders Sr., presiding bishop of United Church of Jesus Christ (Apostolic), were also in attendance.

In 1972, Williams was re-elected chairman, William L. Bonner was elected vice-chairperson, and Nathaniel A. Urshan served as Treasurer. The fellowship held annual meetings throughout the United States from 1963 to 1990; however, the group disbanded following the death of Williams in 1991.

Living Witness of the Apostolic Faith

Healing evangelist Mattie B. Poole and her husband, Charles E. Poole, established Living Witness of the Apostolic Faith (LWAF). The organization was born out of Bethlehem Healing Temple, a congregation established in 1932 within the Pentecostal Assemblies of the World. "Mother Poole's" preaching and healing ministry attracted a large following as reports of healing circulated throughout Chicago and the nation. In 1957 the couple left PAW to join Samuel N. Hancock and the Pentecostal Church of the Apostolic Faith. Sometime after, Charles was elevated to the office of bishop, and after Hancock died in 1963, Mattie and Charles separated and formed Living Witnesses of the Apostolic Faith, Inc.

Through extensive travel, preaching, and conducting healing services, LWAF added congregations in Brooklyn, New York; Boston, Massachusetts; Atlanta, Georgia; Gary, Indiana; Lockport, Illinois; Chicago's Southside and Ghana, Liberia, and Nigeria, West Africa. The Poole's established Living Witness Academy and Theological Seminary in Chicago and several Bible schools in Brooklyn, New York; Atlanta, Georgia; and Boston, Massachusetts.

Mattie passed away in 1968, and Charles served as the presiding bishop until he died in 1984. After his death, the congregation elected Bishop Arcenia C. Richards as pastor of Bethlehem Healing Temple and presider, serving until his death in 2001. In 2006 Chester Hudson was elected pastor of Greater Bethlehem Healing Temple and currently serves in that position. Bishop Clord Jordan succeeded Richards and served from 2001 to 2016. Bishop Melvin Crittenden is the current presiding bishop of the organization. In addition, LWAF has congregations in Illinois, Georgia, Massachusetts, North Carolina, Mississippi, and Quebec, Canada.

Mount Hebron Apostolic Temple of Our Lord Jesus Christ

George H. Wiley organized an Apostle Church of Christ in God church in Yonkers, New York, in 1956. He split with the parent organization in 1963, and Wiley established and incorporated the Mount Hebron Apostolic Temple of Our Lord Jesus Christ. His wife, Lucille, had worked with the ACCG youth department for many years, and the couple developed a following among young African Americans and Latinos.

Within this organization, local congregations are called temples and numbered as they are formed or join the body within the organization. The mother church is Temple No. 1. A second congregation, Temple No. 2, was organized in Manhattan, New York, later in 1963. Finally, in 1978, Temple No. 3 was established by Wiley in Wallace, North Carolina.

By 1979, the organization numbered 3,000 members and ten churches in Greenville, South Carolina, and Sardis, Georgia. Wiley served as the presiding Apostle until 2007. He appointed Bishop Jeremiah Ravenell, who returned to the organization in 2005 as the Presiding Apostle. The two New York congregations merged after Wiley's death in 2008. Mt. Hebron has churches in North Carolina, South Carolina, and Georgia, while its headquarters remains in Yonkers, New York.

Holy Temple Church of the Lord Jesus Christ - 1965

Bishop Randolph Goodwin, a native of Columbia, South Carolina, established the Holy Temple Church of the Lord Jesus Christ (HTCLJC). Goodwin's ministry began under the leadership of Sherrod C. Johnson, the founder of the Church of the Lord Jesus Christ. Goodwin pulled out of the parent body in 1965, starting with five members. Instead, he used his Bronx, New York congregation to launch HTCLJC. In 1967, the newly formed church launched an international radio broadcast ministry that spans Europe, Asia, the Caribbean, and Africa. The organization expanded first to Washington, DC, and Gloucester, Virginia, and by 1987 had six additional congregations throughout Virginia, North Carolina, and Tennessee.

HTCLJC organization does not ordain women preachers and stresses head coverings. The group also discourages the celebration of Christmas, and church members do not receive or give gifts on that occasion. Goodwin led HTCLJC for nearly forty years until he died in 2002. Under his leadership, the organization expanded along the East Coast and the Caribbean, West Africa, and the Philippines.

One of the early charter members, Bishop Belton Green, serves as the Apostle, Pastor, and General overseer. The current membership is 5,200 members with congregations in New York, Florida, California, South Carolina, North Carolina, Tennessee, Virginia, and foreign works in India, the Philippines, Jamaica, Haiti, Trinidad, the Cayman Islands, Nigeria, Ghana, Liberia, and the Democratic Republic of the Congo.

United Church of Jesus Christ (Apostolic)

The organization began under the leadership of Bishop Monroe R. Saunders, Sr. (Baltimore, Maryland); Bishop Sydney A. Dunn (Birmingham, England); Bishop John S. Watson (Jamaica, West Indies); and Bishop Raymond Murray (Boston, Massachusetts). The four bishops had been consecrated leaders in 1957 in the Church of God in Christ Jesus (Apostolic), founded by Bishop Randolph A. Carr. In 1965, the group opposed Carr's decision to break church polity.

The first presiding bishop, Saunders, was assisted by vice bishops, Obediah Colander, Collie Lorick, Charlie Burroughs, and Sydney Dunn. United Church was incorporated in Washington DC, where Saunders pastored. His congregation in Baltimore, Maryland, now known as the Transformation Church, is the organization's headquarters.

By 1980, the organization had fifty-two churches, 150 ministers, and 75,000. Saunders served as the presiding bishop from 1965 until 2004. During the 38th International Convocation in 2004, the organization confirmed him as the Chief Apostle in perpetuity, and his oldest son, Bishop Monroe R. Saunders, Jr., was installed as the presiding prelate.

UCJC is governed by an executive council involving an executive board and a board of bishops, which allows women to serve at all levels of leadership, including as pastor, overseer, and bishop. Currently, four women serve on the board of bishops. The body has congregations across the United States, Canada, England, Jamaica, the Leeward Islands of the West Indies, and Liberia, West Africa.

Cainhoy Miracle Revival Corporation - 1969

Cainhoy Miracle Revival Corporation is one of the few Apostolic organizations established by a woman. The group was founded in 1969 by Apostle Helen Smith, a former member of the Church of Our Lord Jesus Christ of the Apostolic Faith. Smith acknowledged her call to preach in 1968. That year she began with a small group in the home of Mother Moriah Howard of Cainhoy, South Carolina. The revival soon outgrew the home where it was meeting, and the group relocated to a small shack in the same town.

Because Smith's parent organization did not accept the preaching ministry of women, she was asked to end the revival meetings. When Smith did not stop holding the revivals, insisting that God ordained the services, COOLJC excommunicated her and eleven other members. One year after she launched her revival service, Smith was ordained as the Apostle of the Cainhoy Miracle Revival Center.

Under her leadership, the one church grew to fifteen churches in the United States and two churches in Trinidad, West Indies. Smith led the body for thirty years and died in 1999. Bishop Larry Brown, the pastor of Summerville Miracle Revival Center in Summerville, South Carolina congregation, is the organization's current Apostle and Chief Executive Officer. Dr. Velma J.N. Heyward serves as co-chairperson.

Further Reading
Smith, Helen. *You're Going to Be Somebody*. Mobile, AL: Gazelle, 1999.

Apostolic Assemblies of Christ - 1970

One of the five organizations birthed out of Pentecostal Churches of Apostolic Faith. The Detroit-based organization was founded by George N. Boone, who was ordained a bishop in PCAF by Samuel N. Hancock in 1960. Boone withdrew from the organization, starting with seven churches in Michigan, Ohio, and Tennessee. The initial leadership included Virgil Oates, vice-bishop, and Willie Duncan, general secretary. By 1980 the AAOC had grown to twenty-three churches and approximately 3,500 members.

The body is a Covenant Fellowship of pastors governed by a Bishop, an Executive Board, and a Board of Trustees. In addition, women function as licensed and ordained ministers, evangelists, pastors, and jurisdictional and national officers. AAOC reported seventy-seven ordained ministers nationwide in 2008.

Bishop Donald Sorrells was elected presiding bishop in 2012 when Boone moved to the emeritus position. Sorrells founded the Christ Temple Bible College, an accredited and chartered bible school, in 1998. He held the position from 2012 to 2017. After his death, Boone appointed Bramlett Cooper to the office of presiding bishop and Isaac Williams as the assisting presiding bishop. AAOC currently has 259 congregations in California, the South, the Midwest, and parts of the Mid-Atlantic.

United Churches of Jesus, Apostolic

United Churches of Jesus, Apostolic (UCJA) is one of three apostolic bodies established in Winston-Salem, North Carolina, and the second group to be formed because of a split with the Apostle Church of Christ in God. In 1970, several leaders rejected the leadership of ACOCIG's presiding bishop of James. C. Richardson, Sr.

Bishop J. W. Ardrey, one of the founding leaders of the Apostle Church, served as the first general bishop, and James R. Ziglar held the office of vice general bishop. Early pastors were Eli Daniels, Ulyses McCall, S.E. Saunders, Ernest Sanders, and Harley Cotton, with churches in Winston-Salem, Goldsboro, Wilson, Bowden, North Carolina, Hartsville, and Florence, South Carolina.

By 1980 UCJA had 2,000 members, twenty churches, thirty ministers, and six bishops. The organization is governed by a bishop board consisting of bishops and pastors. There are twenty-five churches in North and South Carolina, Virginia, and Alabama, and one congregation in South Africa. Bishop Willie Davis, Jr, is the current general chairman, Bishop Donald Hyman serves as 1st vice-chairman, and Bishop James Millner is the general secretary.

Refuge Temple Assembly of Yahweh

The quasi-Hebrew organization was formed by John W. Pernell, a former leader within the Church of Our Lord Jesus Christ of the Apostolic Faith. Pernell pastored Refuge Temple in Richmond, Virginia, from 1943 to 1969. In 1969, he split with COOLJC over what he considered a "new" revelation concerning the name of Jesus. Pernell believed the Old Testament name Yahweh should be referred to as God rather than the name of Jesus. His refusal to change this position brought about his exclusion from the COOLJC. He resigned from his pastorate to establish a new congregation in Richmond, Refuge Temple Assembly of Yahweh.

Following the formation of Refuge Temple, Pernell ordained twenty-one elders and incorporated his new group. However, he presided over the organization for only one year. After his death in 1971, Refuge set up a board of bishops to govern, and Elmo W. Woodbury founded Refuge Assembly of Yahweh in Norfolk, Virginia, and was appointed presiding bishop. Woodbury served until his death in 2003. Bishop Milton J. Hunt is the current presiding prelate.

Church of Jesus Christ Apostolic, Inc - 1971

Roy C. Williams, a native of Camaguey, Cuba, founded the Church of Jesus Christ Apostolic, Inc in Paterson, New Jersey. His church initially started as a storefront church in 1962. Williams then traveled throughout the East Coast, organizing several congregations. From his base in Paterson, he expanded his ministry into Canada, Jamaica, England, Africa, and India. Afro-Caribbeans make up a large segment of membership in the United States.

In 1973, the organization began publishing The Apostolic Monthly Publication, and two years later, it launched a bible college. COJCA also added the "Apostolic Broadcast" in 1979. Williams led the group for thirty-nine years. Bishop Walter G. McKoy of Englewood, New Jersey, became the presiding bishop after his death in 2010. Arthur G. Brett is the deputy presiding bishop and B. C. Hibbert serves as general secretary.

Evangelistic Churches of Christ of the Apostolic Faith – 1974

Lymus Johnson, an evangelist in the Church of Our Lord Jesus Christ, separated from the group and founded Evangelistic Churches of Christ of the Apostolic Faith in Corona, New York. The congregation grew and was later located in Jackson Heights, New York. When Johnson died in 2012, Bishop Charles Lowe took the position as presider. Today, the organization is no longer governed by one leader but by a presiding body of the Executive Board of Bishops, including Bishop Dwight Daniels, Elder Chuck Taylor, and Bishop Willie Thomas. Congregations are primarily based in New York and Pennsylvania. The organization also has foreign missions in Liberia, Monrovia, and West Africa.

United Way of the Cross Churches of Christ of the Apostolic Faith

The United Way of the Cross Churches of Christ of the Apostolic Faith (UWCCC) was founded by Bishop Joseph Adams, formerly of the Way of the Cross Church of Christ, Elder Harrison J. Twyman of the Bible Way Church of Our Lord Jesus Christ World Wide, and James Pritchard, formerly of the Apostle Church of Christ in God. After formation, the new body had four bishops, thirty ministers, 1,100 members, and fourteen churches. Adams served as the first presiding bishop, and Bishop James H. Carter held the position of vice presiding. In 1998 Carter was elevated as an apostle and appointed chairperson of the Board of Bishops.

After the death of Adam in 2003, he became a presiding bishop and chief executive officer of the Board of Apostles. Carter split with the organization to organize United Cornerstone Churches of Christ International after serving only two years as the presider. UWCCC headquarters is in Danville, Virginia. Approximately fifty churches in North Carolina, South Carolina, Virginia, Maryland, New Jersey, Ohio, and the Caribbean.

Alliance of Apostolic Churches of Christ Jesus – 1977

Alliance of Apostolic Churches of Christ Jesus, a fellowship of ministers formed under the leadership of Albert E. Dixon Sr., a bishop in the Churches of God and True Holiness. After a conversation between Dixon and Bishop Willie Frazier of The New Born Lighthouse Church of the Apostolic Faith, Inc, the fellowship came into existence. A few months later, they shared their vision with Oneness leaders from several small Apostolic bodies and independent congregations. The initial purpose of the fellowship was to teach the doctrines and beliefs of the Apostolic Faith and own, establish, and maintain churches and institutions.

AACCJ was organized initially as the Apostolic Ministerial Alliance in Cleveland, Ohio, where many of its first constituents were. Dixon was elected president, Loyce Clark, vice president, and Raymond Worrell, secretary at the first annual meeting. Pastors from Tennessee, Mississippi, Ohio, Georgia, and Washington, DC joined the fellowship, and later the name was changed to the Alliance of Apostolic Churches of Christ Jesus. Apostle Perry Maples, one of the founding leaders and pastor of Apostolic Deliverance Temple Church in Memphis, Tennessee, is the current presiding president. Bishops J. Timothy Herrington, Raymond Faison, Floyd Nelson, and David Cooper serve on the Executive Board.

Holy Temple Church of Christ - 1979

Bishop Joseph E. Weather served under the pastorate of Bishop Henry C. Brooks, founder of Way of the Cross. After Brooks' death, Weathers appeared most likely to succeed as pastor. Instead, in 1969, presiding bishop John L. Brooks assumed the pastorate of the church. When he did not receive the appointment, Weathers broke away with over one hundred members to form the Holy Temple Church of Christ in Washington, DC. He was consecrated to the office of bishop in 1974 by William L. Bonner, who served as presiding bishop of the Church of Our Lord Jesus Christ. In 1979, he organized Holy Temple Church of Christ and served as the presiding bishop for over thirty years.

Redeemed Assembly of Jesus Christ, Apostolic

James F. Harris and Douglas Williams founded Redeemed Assembly of Jesus Christ, Apostolic after a schismatic break from Highway Christian Church of Christ. The two bishops criticized the then presiding bishop, L. V. Lomax, for his authoritarian style. As a result, they left Highway and began with six congregations in Richmond, Virginia, Washington, DC, and New York. Harris served as the first presiding bishop and Williams as vice bishop. Redeemed Assembly is governed by an executive council involving all the bishops and an executive board consisting of bishops and pastors. Harris has served as presiding prelate for forty-two years.

National Apostolic Fellowship Association - 1987

One of several inter-organizational fellowships was established by Bishop Robert O. Doub, the founder of Shiloh Apostolic Temple Church, Inc, in response to a need for a unified base of Apostolic ministers and churches. As a result, the NAF brought together leaders from various Oneness bodies, including Free Gospel Churches of the Apostles' Doctrine, Way of the Cross Church of Christ, and Holy Temple Church of Christ. The executive officers were Doub as President; Ralph E. Green as Vice-President; Dr. Dennis M. Golphin, Executive Secretary; Overseer William Thomas, Treasurer; and Bishop J. H. Bower, Chaplin.

The organization was incorporated in Maryland in 1992 with Bishops Ralph Green, Alphonzo Brooks, Major Foster, R. H. Prince, and Joseph Weathers as the incorporators. The NAF planned to establish an Apostolic Theological Seminary and develop a construction company to facilitate building churches, schools, and other facilities, give financial and management support to newly forming congregations and establish job creation programs. Today, the current board members include Bishop Major Foster as President; Bishop David Myrick, Sr. as Vice-President; Bishop James Briscoe, Executive Secretary; and Pastor Joseph Lindsay, Treasurer.

Higher Ground Always Abounding Assemblies - 1988

Bishop Sherman S. Watkins, an influential Ohio pastor, organized Higher Ground Always Abounding Assemblies. In 1970 Watkins established Greater Emmanuel Apostolic Church of God, a small storefront with eleven members in Columbus. The membership grew to over 3,000, one of the largest congregations in Columbus, Ohio.

Watkins has served as the presiding prelate for over thirty years. He is a mentor to the famed pastor and televangelist, Bishop Thomas Dexter (T.D.) Jakes, the current vice prelate of the organization. Bishop Glen A. Staples serves as 2nd vice prelate. HGAAA is governed by an Executive Board of Senior Bishops and an Executive Board of Bishops. Headquartered in Columbus, the church has over two hundred congregations throughout the United States, Canada, and foreign missions in the Philippines.

Beth-El Churches of Christ - 1989

The organization was launched in Richmond, Virginia, by Bishop Robert Evans. He served as a bishop and pastor in the Highway Churches of Christ, founded by Raymond F. Davis. From his headquarters in Baltimore, Maryland, Evans sent ministers to establish Beth-El congregations throughout the United States. He served as the presiding bishop for twelve years. Bishop Bernard N. Bragg initially served as interim presider after the death of Evans in 2000. He was officially consecrated as the presiding prelate in 2001. Under his leadership, the organization launched The Beth-El Temple College of Theology (BTCOT) as a North Carolina College of Theology (NCCT) satellite extension.

In 2019, Bishop Richard J. Pender, National Treasurer, was elected as the third Presiding Prelate after the death of Bragg. An episcopal form of government governs Beth-El with five episcopal dioceses led by Pender, bishops Kevin Daniels, Michael D. Chapman, Sr., James B. Smith, and Danny Evans. The organization is open to women serving at all levels of leadership, including bishop, pastor, overseer, and on the executive board. There are congregations throughout Maryland, Massachusetts, North Carolina, Florida, Rhode Island, Delaware, and Pennsylvania.

World Assemblies of Restoration - 1995

Bishop James D. Nelson formed the World Assemblies of Restoration. Before he established WAR, Nelson was baptized in Jesus' name under prominent Pentecostal Assemblies of the World leader Phillip L. Scott in 1963. He later received his Pentecostal Holy Spirit baptism under pastor Grace White. Nelson became the pastor of Greater Bethlehem Temple in Randallstown, Maryland, in 1977 and served for over twenty-five years.

In 1995, Nelson resigned his executive position on the Board of Bishops of the PAW and founded WAR. The organization had grown to more than 300 churches across the United States, West Africa, Jamaica, West Indies, and Canada within a few years. The body's leadership consists of a presiding bishop, an executive board of bishops, a college of bishops, and an executive board.

In 2014, Nelson stepped down from his position of presiding bishop to become presiding bishop emeritus. Jonathan Wallace, who served as the 1st assistant presiding prelate, assumed the presider's office. Nelson returned to the position and is the current presiding bishop. WAR has congregations throughout the United States and an internationally foreign mission department in Liberia, Africa.

Apostolic Faith Fellowship International - 2012

Bishop Charles Johnson, the former bishop of Pentecostal Assemblies of the World, organized Apostolic Faith Fellowship International (AFFI). He succeeded Ramsey N. Butler as the pastor of the Greater Morning Star Apostolic Church in Largo, Maryland. Within PAW, Johnson served as a member of the International Foreign Missions Board, on the Board of Directors for Aenon Bible College, and Chairman of the District of Columbia, Delaware, and Maryland District Council.

He split with PAW in 2012 regarding what he saw as increasing liberalism with the parent body. However, Johnson maintained that he intended to form a fellowship that restored the "doctrine and tenets taught and practiced by the apostolic fathers." When the AFFI held its first national conference in Charlotte, North Carolina, in 2013, Johnson was consecrated as the first presiding bishop, and six pastors were consecrated to the office of bishop. In 2015, the organization launched the AFFI Bible Institute.

The body's leadership consists of a presiding bishop, an executive bishop's council, and a board of bishops. Johnson remains the presiding bishop for the organization with affiliates throughout the United States, the Philippines, and Canada.

Part II:
Pioneers and Leaders

William Charles Abney 1927-2002
Lorraine Elaine Abney

Pastor, community leader, and humanitarian was born in Detroit, Michigan. Abney graduated from Northern High School after returning home from serving a tour of duty in the United States Armed Forces. He graduated from the Detroit Barber College in 1946. Abney received his call to the ministry in 1950. Following his call, he attended Detroit Bible Institute and obtained an associate degree from Bethel Practical School of Theology.

Abney was ordained a minister within Pentecostal Assemblies of the World in 1960. He served as the National Pentecostal Young People's Union and choir director at the Bethel Apostolic Church under the leadership of the late Benjamin J. Goode. Bethel Pentecostal Church in Grand Rapids, Michigan, elected him as pastor in 1961, and after years of growth, the church was renamed Bethel Pentecostal Church Abundant Life Center. Within PAW, he held the diocesan office of the Seventh Episcopal District and bishop emeritus.

Through his ministry, gospel singers Marvin Sapp and Byron Cage and the R & B group the DeBarge Family launched their musical careers. Abney and the Bethel Pentecostal Church Choir recorded an album in 1992. His rendition of the popular gospel song "I Won't Complain" became his signature song.

Abney was a community leader who served on the Board of Directors for the Grand Rapids Chamber of Commerce and as President of the Emmanuel Empowerment Corporation. He also worked on the Campaign Capital Cabinet for the Concern Citizens Council. In 1998, Abney and his wife, Lorraine, founded the William C. Abney Academy, a public charter school that provides tuition-free education for inner-city children.

Joseph H. Adams 1926-2003

The co-founder and first presiding bishop of the United Way of the Cross Churches of Christ was born in Axton, Virginia. He entered the ministry in 1946 and served as associate minister of Shiloh Way of the Cross. Henry C. Brooks ordained him an elder in Way of the Cross Church of Christ in Washington, DC in 1953. He later founded Bethel United Way of the Cross Church of Christ in Danville, Virginia. In 1969, he was consecrated to the office of bishop under the leadership of John Luke Brooks, the second presiding bishop. After his appointment to the bishopric, Adams served as diocesan bishop over the state of North Carolina. In 1974, Adams split with WOTCC.

Along with Harrison Twyman, former Bible Way Church of Our Lord Jesus Christ leader, and James Pritchard of the Apostle Church of Christ in God, he organized the United Way of the Cross Churches of Christ. By 1980, the organization had over 1,100 members and fourteen churches throughout Virginia, North Carolina, and Maryland.

Adams earned his theology degrees from the Staunton Bible Institute and the Shiloh School of Theology in Stafford, Virginia. His leadership extended beyond his local church and organization. From 1970 to 1990, he served on the Henry County School Board, including vice-chairperson. He was also a chartered member and vice-chairperson of the Sandy River Medical Center Board. In addition, Adams founded the Bethel Way Adult Center and the Bethel Way Recreation Center. He was appointed to the Governor's Advisory Board for the Aging by Virginia's first African American governor, Douglas Wilder. In 2004, after his death, the Virginia State Senate and the House of Delegates passed a state resolution that recognized his outstanding service as a community leader in Virginia.

Elmer Fremont Akers 1897-1980

Elmer F. Akers served as General Secretary and bishop in Pentecostal Assemblies of the World. Akers was born in Hiawatha, Kansas. He was ordained minister in PAW in 1920 and traveled as an evangelist, preaching throughout the South and Midwest. In 1922, he led a highly successful revival at the First Pentecostal Church in Dayton, Ohio. As a result, the congregation asked him to assume the church's pastorate, later renamed Bethesda Temple Church.

He rose to prominence in PAW after the death of G. T. Haywood in 1931. In March 1932, a special meeting was held at Akers' church in Dayton to reorganize the organization. As a result, Samuel J. Grimes was elected the second presiding bishop of PAW, and Akers became the General Secretary at this meeting. One year after his election to the office of general secretary, PAW appointed him to the office of bishop. Akers left PAW in 1946 and joined the Church of God in Christ Jesus Apostolic, founded by Randolph A. Carr, where he held the office of General Secretary. He also pastored churches in Brooklyn, New York, and Bloomington, Indiana.

J. W. Ardrey Sr. 1911-1982

One of the founding leaders and the first presiding bishop of the Apostle Church of Christ was initially an elder in the Church of God, Apostolic, founded by Thomas J. Cox. Ardrey served as pastor of St. Paul Apostolic Church in Rudd, North Carolina, near Greensboro. In 1941, he and four other elders, James C. Richardson, Jerome Jenkins, W. R. Bryant, and J. M. Williams, separated from COGA. Ardrey, the senior elder of the group, was appointed presiding bishop. He resigned from the position in 1956, and in 1970, he and several ministers left ACCG. The group established the United Churches of Jesus Christ, Apostolic. His organization has over twenty-five congregations throughout North Carolina, South Carolina, Virginia, Alabama, and one church in South Africa.

George Washington Ayers 1927-2015
Verley Mildred Ayers 1928-2014

The third presiding bishop of Apostolic Overcoming Holy Church of God was born in Maben, Alabama. At the age of eighteen, he enlisted in the United States Army and served in World War II in 1945. He was awarded a Purple Heart after being wounded on the Island of Guam. He accepted his call to ministry, married Verley Mildred Smith, and joined Apostolic Overcoming Holy Church in Tuskegee, Alabama. After that, Ayers moved to Marin City, California, and founded the "first" AOHC church.

In 1953 he received a B.A. degree in Business from Booker T. Washington Business College in Birmingham, Alabama, then received a TH.B. degree from Bethel School of Theology, Detroit, Michigan, in 1957. In 1977, he received TH.M., a degree from Maranatha Bible College, Union, South Carolina, a TH.D in 1990, and a Ph.D. in theology in 1994. He was also awarded the D.D. and L.L.D from the International Bible Institute and Seminary, Orlando, Florida.

He was appointed an Overseer and a member of the AOHC executive board in 1956. In 1965, Ayers was consecrated to the office of bishop. He was elected presiding bishop by the National

Executive Board after the second presiding bishop, Jasper Roby, became ill and could no longer serve in the office in 2000. A legal battle followed his election when a fraction of AOHC leaders disagreed with his appointment. The Supreme Court of Alabama named Ayers the rightful leader of AOHC in 2002.

Ayers pastored the Cathedral of the Cross AOHC Church of God in Birmingham, AL, and Phillips Temple AOHC Church of God in Mobile, AL. He also served as a community activist in Marin City. He supported hiring the city's first African American police officers and established a ministerial alliance that dealt with complaints of police brutality. Ayers and his wife, Verley, pastored Faith Tabernacle AOH Church of God for fifty-eight years.

Oddous Barber 1888-1966

Born in Danville, Kentucky, in 1888, the early Pentecostal leader was instrumental in the growth of the Apostolic movement in Boston, Massachusetts. His family moved to Indianapolis, Indiana, sometime after 1900, and he attended Apostolic Faith Assembly under the leadership of Henry Prentiss in 1907. He and his brother were close friends with Garfield T. Haywood. Oddous convinced young Haywood to attend his church. After Haywood heard Prentiss preach the Pentecostal message of Spirit baptism, he received the baptism of the Holy Spirit.

Prentiss left Apostolic Faith Assembly in 1909, and Haywood took over as pastor. Barber served as an assistant pastor. In 1925, he organized Christ Temple, one of the first PAW churches in Boston. Barber worked closely with minister C. R. Wilkes, who also established works in Boston and Roxbury, Massachusetts. Around 1940, Barber organized Christ Temple of Personal Experience in Roxbury with prominent black minister Reverend W. Frederick Fisher. Finally, Barber moved back to Indianapolis, where he would live the remainder of his life.

John D. Barnes 1914-1980
Rosa Barnes

Pentecostal Assemblies of the World leader in the Mid-Atlantic served as assistant pastor at Greater Bethlehem Temple Church in Detroit, Michigan, under Samuel N. Hancock for fifteen years. He moved from Detroit to Baltimore, Maryland, in 1942. That year he took over as pastor of Bethlehem Temple after the departure of Norman D. Bridges.

Barnes was appointed a District Elder in PAW with Winfield A. Showell and Ramsey N. Butler in 1950. He served as chairman of the auditing committee of PAW and was a member of the DC, Delaware, and Maryland District Council (formerly known as the Eastern District Council). Barnes held the position of Vice Chairman and Treasurer. His wife, Rosa, served as an evangelist and missionary in the council for many years. Barnes pastored Bethlehem Temple for over thirty years.

William Samuel Barnes 1909-1987

The second presiding bishop of the Church of God in Christ Jesus Apostolic, Barnes was a native of Baltimore, Maryland. He grew up in the Methodist tradition but later joined First Apostolic Faith Church under the pastorate of Joseph M. Turpin in the 1920s. Barnes met and married Geneva Johnson in 1928. He accepted the pastorate of Mt. Zion Church of the First Born in 1946. A few months later, he founded St. Paul Apostolic Faith Church and affiliated with the Church of God in Christ Jesus Apostolic.

Randolph A. Carr appointed him Overseer of the Southern District. He was consecrated to the office of bishop in 1967, and following the death of Carr in 1970, Barnes assumed the pastorate of Rehoboth Church of God in Christ Jesus and became presiding bishop. He established the International Women's Council and the International Brotherhood. Most significantly, he appointed women as voting members of the Governing Board. Barnes led the organization for over seventeen years.

Ralph Bass 1893-1972

The influential Pentecostal Assemblies of the World leader was born in West Jefferson, Ohio. In his early ministry, he served as pastor of El Bethel Temple in Springfield, Ohio, for sixteen years. Bass was appointed a District Elder in 1932 and held the office for thirty years. In 1936, he took over the pastorate of Bethesda Temple in Dayton, Ohio. PAW elevated him to the position of bishop in 1959, and he was assigned diocesan over the State of Arkansas. Bass held the diocesan of the Ohio District Council after the resignation of Karl F. Smith in 1970. He served as pastor of Bethesda Temple for thirty-six years.

Sidney Coy Bass 1899-1977

Sidney Coy Bass was born to former slaves in Durham, North Carolina. His family moved to Mount Hope, West Virginia, and he became one of the early converts of the Black Nationalist group, Triumph the Church and Kingdom of God in Christ, led by Elias D. Smith. In 1918, Bass accepted the call to preach, and by the 1920s though still in his twenties, he served as a leader on the State Board of Triumph the Church.

In 1921, after Triumph the Church and Kingdom of God in Christ was reorganized as Glorious Church of God in Christ, Albart Smith was appointed the first General Overseer. GCOGIC adopted baptism in Jesus' name that same year however, Bass rejected the teaching but was later convinced by Mother Lulu Phillips

Upon the death of Smith in 1928, Bass became presiding elder and pastor of the headquarters church in Huntington, West Virginia. In 1944, he was appointed the first General Bishop of GCOGIC. The organization split in 1952 after he married a divorced woman. Approximately half of the churches rejected his leadership and reorganized it as the Original Glorious Church of God in Christ Apostolic Faith. However, Bass continued to preside over the parent organization for 33 years. In 1977, he died following an automobile accident in Roanoke, Virginia.

John Solomon Beane 1888-1973
Miranda Beane 1890-1971

One of the five founders of Bible Way Church of Our Lord Jesus was born in Virginia in 1892. He joined and became an ordained minister in Churches of Christ of the Apostolic Faith under the leadership of Robert C. Lawson sometime before 1924. After his ordination, Beane organized Bethesda Church of Christ in Petersburg, Virginia. He served as State Overseer, and his wife Miranda Beane worked as the National Chairlady of the Women's Council in COOLJC.

In 1957, Beane split with COOLJC and became the founding bishop of Bible Way Church Our Lord Jesus Christ World Wide, Inc., along with Smallwood E. Williams, Winfield A. Showell, Joseph Moore, and McKinley Williams. His church hosted Bible Way World Wide's first annual Bishops' and Workers' Council Conference in March 1958. In addition, mother Beane served as National Chairlady of the Missionary Department. As one of the founding leaders of Bible Way, he served as the first vice-bishop, first treasurer, and diocesan of the Virginia State Diocese until he died in 1973.

Dennis Rayford Bell 1923-2013

D. Rayford Bell served as the presiding bishop of Pentecostal Churches of the Apostolic Faith from 1989 to 2000. The son of sharecroppers, Bell, was born in Leflore County, Mississippi. He was drafted into the Army and sent to Europe to fight in World War II. Bell received the baptism of the Holy Spirit a few years after his honorable discharge from military service in 1945. He joined Christ Temple Church in Chicago, Illinois, a congregation affiliated with PCAF, founded by Samuel N. Hancock in 1957.

Bell took over as pastor of Christ Temple after the death of Samuel Barnes in 1958. He was ordained as a District Elder in 1961 and appointed to the office of bishop in 1964. As a leader in PCAF, he established the Midwest Apostolic Bible College and founded Samuel Barnes Christian Academy. Bell also worked as a Chaplain for the Chicago Police Department. In 1990, he succeeded Elzie Young as the presiding bishop of PCAF and served as the leader for ten years.

Isaiah W. Bollinger 1910-1976
Catherine Bollinger 1911-1993

Isaiah and Catherine Bollinger were prominent leaders of the Church of Our Lord Jesus Christ and the Bible Way Church of Our Lord Jesus Christ. Born in Cape Girardeau, Missouri, Bollinger was ordained a minister in the COOLJC sometime in the 1930s. Bishop Robert C. Lawson sent him to pastor Refuge Church of Christ in Atlanta, Georgia. In 1941, a young man named William L. Bonner walked into the Refuge Church while Bollinger was preaching and asked to be baptized in Jesus' name. Bonner would become the third presiding bishop of COOLJC. In 1946, Bollinger became the pastor of Bible Way Church of Christ; a church started as a small prayer band founded by Dorthula Norwood, Gladys Smith, and Fannie Norwood. Bollinger joined the Bible Way Church of Our Lord Jesus Christ in 1960 and became an influential leader of the Bible Way movement and contributed to the formation of the Georgia Diocese.

Ethel Mae Smith Bonner 1918-1999

Educator, women's leader, missionary, and social advocate became the wife of William L. Bonner, third and longest-serving presiding bishop of the Church of Our Lord Jesus Christ of the Apostolic Faith, Inc. Born in New York City, Ethel Smith attended Refuge Temple in Harlem and served as secretary for Robert C. Lawson, the founder of the Church of Our Lord Jesus Christ. In 1944, Ethel met and married William L. Bonner. Lawson sent William to pastor a small storefront church in Detroit, Michigan, in 1946. Ethel supported her husband's ministry and managed their restaurant, Bonner's Kitchen, from 1946 to 1950.

Bonner studied at Union Theological Seminary in New York but later earned a Bachelor of Arts degree from Hunter College. She received her Master of Arts degree from Wayne State University in Detroit, Michigan, and an honorary Doctor of Sacred Letters from American Wesleyan College of the Northern Educational and Theological Consortium.

In Detroit, Bonner taught languages and social sciences for Detroit Public Schools. For over thirty years, she promoted the cause of private education within the Christian community and directed private school programs within COOLJC. Also, she served as an educational consultant for the Detroit systems and Wayne

State University. In addition, Bonner spent three years in Liberia, West Africa, teaching and organizing a school and dormitories and initiating projects for teacher training.

A pioneer leader in COOLJC, Bonner organized the Ministers and Deacons Wives Guild to provide training and fellowship for the women who supported their husband's ministry and leadership. As president, she established the monthly magazine, *The Apostolic Women*. Bonner was appointed the executive director of the 24,000-member International Association of Ministers Wives and Minister's Widows, Inc. in 1984 because of her influential leadership. Although Bonner separated from William, she remained a part of COOLJC. Before her death in 1999, Bonner received the Spirit of Detroit Award and a Special Recognition Award by the President of Liberia for her mission work in Liberia.

Further Readings:
Bonner, Ethel. *This is My Story*. Unpublished manuscript.

Williams, Pandora. *Outstanding Women and their Contributions to the Church of Our Lord Jesus Christ of the Apostolic Faith,* Inc. S.l.: International Missionary Department, 1994.

William Lee Bonner 1921-2015

Apostolic father, pastor, preacher, educator, and third presiding bishop of the Church of Our Lord Jesus Christ was born in Bolden County, Georgia. In 1941, Bonner encountered baptism in Jesus' name at Refuge Church in Atlanta under the leadership of Elder Isaiah Bollinger. His ministry began a few months later under the tutelage of COOLJC founder Robert C. Lawson, for whom he served as a chauffeur and key aide. His first pastorate was the Green Avenue Church of Our Lord Jesus Christ in Brooklyn, New York.

In 1944, William met and married Ethel Mae Smith, and two years later, Lawson sent him to pastor the First Church of Our Jesus Christ in Detroit, Michigan. The small storefront renamed Solomon's Temple grew to seat over twenty-five hundred people. In 1961, Bonner was elected to the three-person board of presiding bishops with Hubert J. Spencer and Maurice Hutner after Lawson's death, but at the same time, he took over the 3,000-member mother church in New York. While he served as pastor of two mega-churches, Bonner founded churches in Washington, DC, and Jackson, Mississippi.

Refuge Temple, established by Bonner in Columbia, South Carolina, in 1993, grew to over seven hundred members. He also organized Refuge Temple Family Life Center, Adult Community Apartment Complex, W. L from this church. Bonner College, and the R. C. Lawson Library. In Bokaytown, Liberia, West Africa, he built a maternal clinic for women from the "Bush" to have their babies in healthy and sanitary conditions.

Bonner was elevated to the presiding prelate of COOLJC after the death of Hubert Spencer in 1973 and served as presider for over forty years. Under his administration, the organization grew from 155 churches to over 500 churches throughout the United States, Africa, and the United Kingdom. In 1989, Bonner was appointed Chief Apostle of COOLJC. He vacated the presiding bishop to Gentle Groover in 1995 but remained the Chief Apostle until his death at age ninety-three in 2015.

Further Reading:
W. L. Bonner Literary Committee. *And the High Places I'll Bring Down: Bishop William L. Bonner, the Man and His God.* Detroit, MI: W. L. Bonner Literary Committee, 1999.

George Marshall Boone 1920-2018
Mae Dee Boone 1923-2018

The founder and first presiding bishop of Apostolic Assemblies of Christ, Inc. was born in Myrtle, Mississippi. Boone grew up during the Great Depression and at the height of the Jim Crow era. Though Boone came to the Christian faith at an early age, while serving in the military in New Guinea, he received the baptism of the Holy Spirit through the witness of a Church of God in Christ pastor.

Boone returned to his hometown after completion of military service in 1946 and married Mae Dee Lockhart. The same year, he embraced the Apostolic doctrine, and his family moved to Detroit, Michigan, where he joined the Pentecostal Churches of the Apostolic faith. Boone served as assistant pastor under Heardie Leaston and was ordained to the office of elder by Samuel N. Hancock in 1961. He also served as a District Elder and chairman of the Michigan State Council.

In 1964, Boone established New Liberty Apostolic Faith Church in Detroit. One year later, in 1965, the Board of Bishops elevated him to the office of bishop. In 1970, he left PCAF to organize the Apostolic Assemblies of Christ, Inc., starting with seven churches in Michigan, Ohio, and Tennessee. Within years, the organization expanded to over 3,500 members and twenty-five churches in Alabama, Arkansas, California, Florida, Georgia, Illinois, Indiana, Kentucky, Louisiana, Mississippi, Missouri, North Carolina, South Carolina, Texas, Liberia, and Haiti. Boone presided over AAOC for forty-two years until he stepped down in 2012 and became bishop emeritus.

Frank Reuben Bowdan 1910-1976
Viola Bernice Bowdan 1903-1981

Pentecostal Assemblies of the World bishop and leader was born in Los Angeles, California, to early Azusa Street Revival eyewitnesses Maggie and William S. Bowdan. Frank received the baptism of the Holy Spirit at Belvedere Gospel Tabernacle in Los Angeles under the leadership of early Oneness Pentecostal leader Frank J. Ewart. He and his family later joined Apostolic Faith Home Assembly under the pastorate of William A. Carson. At age ten, Bowdan was called to the ministry a year later and conducted his first tent revival in Pasadena, California.

In 1930, he moved to Indianapolis, where Bishop Garfield T. Haywood mentored him, and he was ordained shortly after in PAW. In 1934, Bowdan married Viola Bernice Horner. His first pastorate was at Glad Tidings Mission in Chicago, Illinois Chicago, where he served for sixteen months. In 1936, upon the recommendation of Samuel N. Hancock, he became the pastor of Bethlehem Temple Church in Flint, Michigan. He served there for fifteen years until he was called to pastor the Apostolic Faith Home Assembly in Los Angeles after PAW leader Floyd I. Douglas in 1951. The membership quickly increased under his pastorate.

Bowdan's rise through the ranks of the PAW leadership began in 1947 when he became Assistant General Secretary. While still in that position, he was elevated to suffragan bishop in 1959, then to a full bishop in 1962. A few years later, he was elected bishop over the California Nevada District Council. In 1968, Bowdan held the assistant presiding bishop, serving under presiding bishop Ross Paddock and holding that office until 1974. In 1972, when the West Coast Branch of Aenon Bible College expanded in Los Angeles, Bowdan was selected as president. He served as president of the Aenon School of Theology until he died in 1976.

Further Reading:
LeBlanc, Deborah Sims. *Like a Rose ...: Life, Times, and Messages of the Late Bishop Frank R. Bowdan, D.D. 1910-1976.* Los Angeles, CA: DLB Associates, 1989.

Maggie Bowdan, 1884-1929
William S. Bowdan 1875-1935

She was one of the early African American women to attend and receive the experience of Pentecostal Holy Spirit baptism at the Azusa Street Revival. Maggie and her husband, William, joined Belvedere Gospel Tabernacle, pastored by Oneness Pentecostal pioneer Frank Ewart. In 1913, she attended the Arroyo Seco Camp Meeting and embraced water baptism in Jesus' name.

The family left Belvedere Gospel and became early chartered Apostolic Faith Home Assembly members in Los Angeles. Bowdan traveled throughout California, the Midwest, and the Southwest as an evangelist and preacher. In September 1929, following a successful evangelistic tour in Sacramento, she became seriously ill and died at forty-five. Her son, Frank R. Bowdan, became the pastor of the Apostolic Faith Home Assembly in 1951 and he served as the president of the West Coast Branch of Aenon Bible College in Los Angeles.

Further Reading:
Pentecostal Assemblies of the World. *The Christian Outlook Magazine*. Indianapolis, IN: Pentecostal Assemblies of the World, 1929.

Paul Alexander Bowers 1929-2019

A native of Oxford, Pennsylvania, the former presiding bishop of the Pentecostal Assemblies of the World known as the "Preaching Machine" was called to preach in 1942. He assumed the pastorate of Emanuel Apostolic Temple in Cincinnati, Ohio, in 1956. While pastoring, Bowers attended Xavier University and the University of Cincinnati, earning a Bachelor of Science Degree. He taught Social Studies in the Cincinnati Public School System and retired in 1968. Bowers was elected General Secretary within PAW and served until 1976. That same year, he was elevated to the bishopric and assigned Diocesan of the Carolina State Council. Churches in the council grew from 30 to 62 during his twenty years of leadership.

The organization appointed him Chairman of the Ohio District Council in 1973. Under his administration, the district council constructed a new 1.5-million-dollar Nursing Home for the elderly. He also helped to develop the ODC Campground in Zanesville, Ohio. Bowers was elevated to the office of presiding bishop in 1992. He spearheaded a massive remodeling project of the PAW International Headquarters in Indianapolis, Indiana, and served as the presider from 1992 to 1998.

Bernard Nathaniel Bragg 1948-2019

The second presiding bishop of Beth-El Churches of Christ was born in Randallstown, Maryland. He was ordained in 1986 under the leadership of Bishop Robert Evans, the founder of Beth-El Churches of Christ. Along with a Bachelor of Science and Master of Arts degrees in special education from Coppin State College in Baltimore, Maryland, Bragg holds two honorary doctorate degrees. He worked in the Baltimore City Public School System as a teacher and administrator throughout much of his ministry before retiring to fulfill his duties as bishop in 2000.

Bragg pastored the New Life Restoration Temple in Boston, Massachusetts, and served as the organization's General Secretary. He was consecrated to the office of bishop in 1999. In 2001, after the death of Evans, Bragg was elected the presiding prelate of Beth-El Churches of Christ. Under his direction, the organization expanded in Maryland, Massachusetts, Pennsylvania, and Florida.

In addition to his work in Beth-El Churches, Bragg served on the Board of Directors of Umoja House, a home for troubled young people, and the Healing Our Land Ministries, a ministry for men and women with HIV and AIDS. Named in the Who's Who Among American Pastors, he directed the Apostolic Constituent for Women Pastors Alliance, a fellowship designed to mentor and promote women, pastors. Bragg unexpectedly died while attending the Joint College of African American Bishops Annual Meeting in Cleveland, Ohio, in 2019.

Arthur Monroe Brazier 1921-2010
Esther Isabelle Brazier 1929-

Pastor, bishop, community activist, and social justice advocate was born in Chicago and grew up on the city's south side during the Great Depression. Brazier was drafted into the Army in 1942 after America entered World War II. He served in the military for three years. Upon his return, he married Esther Isabelle and was baptized in Jesus' name under the pastorate of Elder Herbert C. Moore. He later joined the Universal Church of Christ, which his mother, Geneva, headed. Brazier answered the call to ministry in 1948 and, not long afterward, became assistant pastor of his mother's congregation. Three years after her death in 1949, he assumed her pastorate, enrolling in Moody Bible Institute in 1955 for formal preparation for ministry.

In 1960, he was asked to pastor the Apostolic Church of God in Chicago's Woodlawn community. Brazier merged this congregation with the smaller Universal Church of Christ. Eventually, the congregation would grow from 100 members to over 20,000. As a PAW member, Brazier served as Secretary of the Convention Committee. He was elevated to the bishopric in 1976 and served as diocesan bishop of the Illinois 6th Episcopal District for over thirty years.

Brazier's civic accomplishments included the Woodlawn Organization, which opposed the expansion of the University of Chicago and the displacement of black Woodlawn residents in 1963. He also served as founder and chair of the Woodlawn Preservation and Investment Corporation, a group that acquired vacant city property on which it built low- and mixed-income housing. In addition, as chair and vice president of the Center of Community Change, a Washington DC-based organization, he provided technical assistance to the Community Development Corporation on large-scale housing and commercial projects throughout the United States.

He worked with the Civil Rights leader, Dr. Martin Luther King. In 1966, Brazier invited King to Chicago to protest segregation in housing and education. Brazier left PAW after seventy-five years of service in 2007. He stepped down as pastor to become emeritus in 2008, turning over the reins to his son, Byron T. Brazier. In that same month, he was named the first senior fellow of the Chicago branch of the Local Initiatives Support Corporation. President Barack Obama acknowledged Brazier's work as a social activist and civil rights leader at his death. He called Brazier "one of our nation's leading moral lights" and "a committed patriot."

Further Readings:

Brazier, Arthur M, Larry Crowe, and Matthew Hickey. The Historymakers Video Oral History with Bishop Arthur Brazier, 2016.

Dortch, Sammie M. *When God Calls: A Biography of Bishop Arthur M. Brazier*. Grand Rapids, MI: W.B. Eerdmans, 1996.

Peter Jan F. Bridges 1890-1962

Born in Washington, North Carolina, the early Pentecostal Assemblies of the World leader grew up in the Methodist church, but he later joined the Holiness Movement. Like many African Americans, Bridges migrated from the South to the North after World War I. Shortly after, he convinced his childhood friend, Frank Clemmons, to relocate to New York. Clemmons would go on to establish the historic First Church of God in Christ in Brooklyn.

Bridges embraced the Apostolic doctrine and was baptized by Garfield T. Haywood in Columbus, Ohio. He joined PAW sometime before 1919, but soon after, he joined the Church of Christ of the Apostolic Faith under the leadership of Robert C. Lawson in 1920. While in Lawson's organization, Bridges traveled as an evangelist, preaching throughout the east coast and establishing churches in Coney Island and Brooklyn, New York.

He rejoined PAW sometime after 1925, and three years later, in 1928, Bridges was appointed a District Elder and named a delegate of the Eastern District Council. He also served as the District Elder over Long Island and Connecticut. Bridges resigned from PAW in 1933 and again rejoined COOLJC. In 1938, he established a second church, Beulah Church of Our Lord Jesus

Christ, in Bedford-Stuyvesant in Brooklyn. He pastored Beulah for twenty-six years.

In 1946, Bridges separated from COOLJC and affiliated with the Church of God in Christ Jesus Apostolic, founded by Randolph A. Carr. Once there, he served as General Treasurer and Diocesan bishop over New York, Maryland, Delaware, Washington, DC, Florida, South Carolina, North Carolina, and Virginia. He remained in the Church of God in Christ Jesus Apostolic until he died in 1962.

Further Readings:
Pentecostal Assemblies of the World. *The Christian Outlook Magazine.* Indianapolis, IN: Pentecostal Assemblies of the World, 1933.

Taylor, Clarence. *The Black Churches of Brooklyn.* New York: Columbia University Press, 1994.

George Harold Brooks 1897-1993
Nellie Brooks 1904-1992

One of the prominent bishops in Pentecostal Assemblies of the World was born in Brunswick, Maryland. Brooks served in the United States Army in World War I. He was ordained a Baptist minister and attended seminary in Pittsburgh, Pennsylvania, until 1924. That year, He and his wife Nellie accepted water baptism and filled with the Holy Ghost at Gospel Tabernacle, under the Pastorate of Elder Charles Johnson in Havre De Grace, Maryland.

Brooks relocated to Waterbury, Connecticut, in 1936. There he became the pastor of Star of Bethlehem in Ansonia, Connecticut. In 1950, Brooks replaced Lambert Tolbert as pastor of the Beulah Heights First Pentecostal Church in New Haven. He worked closely with the second presiding Samuel J. Grimes. For a short time, he served as Grimes's chauffeur. Brooks was appointed a District Elder in 1940 and elected Suffragan bishop in 1958.

His work in Connecticut led to his promotion to the bishopric and the Connecticut District Council leader in

1964. In addition, he served on the Board of Directors of Aenon Bible College and received an honorary Doctor of Divinity from the school. In 1987, Brooks retired as pastor of Beulah Heights First Pentecostal Church. His son, Theodore L. Brooks, succeeded him as the pastor and now serves as the current presiding bishop of PAW.

Henry Chauncey Brooks 1896-1967
Willie Shaw Brooks 1897-1989

The Founder of Way of the Cross Church of Christ was born in Franklinton, North Carolina. He and his sister Lenora Hamilton moved to Washington, DC, after the death of their father in 1912. Brooks joined the United States Navy and served in World War I at the age of twenty-one. He married Willie Shaw Dunston after his honorable discharge from the Navy. In 1925 while affiliated with a Baptist congregation in the city, Brooks attended a Oneness Pentecostal revival intending to disrupt it and persuade the preacher of the error of his ways. However, by the time the altar call was made, Brooks had a change of mind, and he was converted to the Pentecostal faith and baptized by in Jesus' name during the meeting. Meanwhile, he continued attending the Baptist Church until excommunicated several months later.

Brooks established a church with a membership of four people in 1927. The church initially held services in the home of Charles and Alice Johnson. Here, John Bruce, a deacon, penned the church's name, "The Way of the Cross." Many flocked to the Apostolic message preached by Brooks. The membership quickly grew, and soon after, the congregation moved into a larger building.

At the time, Way of the Cross was an independent church, not affiliated with any organization. Brooks traveled to Baltimore, Maryland, hoping to join PAW, but the organization rejected his request. A few months later, James T. Morris, the founder of Highway Christian Church, introduced Brooks to Robert C. Lawson. In 1928, the Way of the Cross became a charted church under the Church of Christ of the Apostolic Faith. That same year, Lawson ordained Brooks to the office of elder.

In 1933, Brooks established the Way of the Cross Church of Christ and incorporated the organization. Brooks served as the presiding bishop from 1933 to 1967. Membership reached over 3,000, with twenty-five churches spread throughout Washington, DC, Maryland, North Carolina, South Carolina, New York, Pennsylvania, and internationally in Haiti, the Dominican Republic, and West Africa.

John Luke Brooks, 1896-1981
Laura B. Brooks 1897-1979

The second presiding bishop of Way of the Cross Church of Christ was born one of seventeen children in Franklinton, North Carolina. He attended Shaw University in Raleigh, North Carolina. A few years later, he joined the United States Army and served in World War I in 1918. Brooks embraced the revelations of Jesus' name and was baptized at Way of the Cross in Washington, DC, in 1936. After ministering for eight years in Lorain, Ohio, he returned to his hometown to pastor Ransom Way of the Cross.

Seven years after his consecration to the bishopric, Brooks returned to Washington, DC, and succeeded his brother-in-law, Henry C. Brooks, as the presiding bishop of the organization in 1967. He also assumed the pastorate of "the mother church" in 1969. Brooks implemented several new initiatives during his tenure. He established a Founders Week, a Board of Bishops, and a Pastoral Council. He also planted congregations in Ghana, West Africa. Brooks served as presiding for fourteen years.

Henry H. Brown 1914-1972
Minnie L. Brown 1915-1995

The early leader of Bible Way Church of Our Lord Jesus Christ joined Bible Way Church in Washington, DC, under the leadership of Smallwood E. Williams in 1941. After many years of service at Bible Way Church, Henry and Mother Minnie Brown organized Bible Way Church#2 in Prince Frederick, Maryland, as part of the Church of Our Lord Jesus Christ in 1952. He joined Bible Way World Wide, founded by Williams, in 1957.

A few years later, Brown was assigned District Elder over the District of Columbia. Next, Williams appointed him to the office of Junior Bishop and Diocesan over Prince Frederick, MD, Eastern North Carolina, and South Carolina Diocese in 1962. Finally, Brown was consecrated to the office of the bishop at the 13th Convocation held in Washington, DC, in 1970. He served as a member of the Executive Board of Bishops and Presiding Officer of Foreign Missions. Brown carried the Apostolic message to Africa, France, England, and Jamaica.

Ramsey Nathaniel Butler 1906-1998
Minnie Brown Butler 1915-1995

Ramsey N. Butler was born in 1906 in Saluda, South Carolina. Butler's family moved to the District of Columbia in 1923. He remarried in 1938 after the death of his first wife, Irene. Butler married Minnie Brown, wife of the late Bishop Henry Brown, in 1977 after his second wife, Martha, died. He entered the ministry in 1932 and served as assistant pastor of Highway Church of Christ under James T. Morris, who was affiliated with Pentecostal Assemblies of the World.

In 1935, a small group of Highway members met in the home of Amelia Williams. From this prayer band, she organized what later became known as Morning Star Pentecostal Church. Butler was installed as pastor of the small congregation after the death of Williams in 1936. Within PAW, he served as chairman of the DC, Delaware, and Maryland District Council. He led the council until 1971. As Morning Star Church grew, Butler undertook an extensive construction program adding the Ramsey N. Butler educational building. He retired in 1986 and held the title Bishop Emeritus in PAW until he died in 1998.

Lucille Tanzella Calloway 1924-2021

One of the longest-serving Apostolic female pastors in the United States was born in Litwar, West Virginia. The granddaughter of slaves, she was the first in her family to graduate from high school. Lucille married Leon Calloway in 1945 and moved to Baltimore, Maryland. During the time, she received the Baptism of the Holy Spirit after hearing Bishop Winfield A. Showell, the pastor of First Apostolic Faith Church, on his weekly radio broadcast.

In 1947, Calloway became the pastor of Faith Tabernacle Apostolic Church, a small storefront church located in the historic Turner Station in Baltimore. The congregation grew despite the challenges of serving as a woman pastor in the Apostolic faith. Calloway battled and was healed of breast cancer in 1975. Following in 1980, she became the first woman to be appointed to the Governing Board of the Church of God in Christ Jesus, Apostolic under Presiding Bishop William S. Barnes. Calloway also served as Vice Presiding bishop of Victorious Apostolic Churches. She pastored her Faith Tabernacle Apostolic Church in East Baltimore until ninety-seven.

Randolph Adolphus Carr 1896-1970

The founder of the Church of God in Christ Jesus Apostolic was born in 1896 in Nevis, West Indies. Carr migrated from the Caribbean to London and later to New York in 1912. He received his early education in the West Indies and attended Northwestern Theological Seminary in Chicago, Illinois. Carr was baptized in the name of Jesus under the leadership of Susan Lightford, the founder of King's Chapel Assembly in Harlem. He joined Pentecostal Assemblies of the World, traveling as an evangelist throughout the West and Midwest. In 1919, Carr was excommunicated from PAW for unknown reasons.

He affiliated with the Church of God in Christ in 1931 in Philadelphia, Pennsylvania. In 1934, Charles H. Mason, the founder of COGIC, sent Carr to Baltimore, Maryland, to pastor the Church of God#6, founded by Mother Emily Mayfield. That same year, a new building was purchased and dedicated by O. T. Jones, one of the first five bishops of COGIC.

He held several successful summer tent revivals, then purchased three-row houses, expanding his church. In 1945, a dispute arose between Carr and COGIC over the issue of baptism in Jesus' name. COGIC, a Pentecostal Trinitarian group, practiced baptism in the name of the Father, Son, and Holy Ghost. Before joining COGIC, Carr adhered to Oneness Pentecostal beliefs. Following his dispute, he organized the Church of God in Christ Jesus Apostolic, and he renamed his local congregation, Rehoboth Church of God, in Christ Jesus Apostolic. Carr presided over the body and pastored Rehoboth until he died in 1970. COGCJA, the organization he founded, has congregations throughout the United States, Canada, Jamaica, Bermuda, and Great Britain.

William A. Carson

Carson was one of the first African Americans to organize an Apostolic church in Los Angeles, California. A native of Chicago, Illinois, he traveled as Pentecostal Assemblies of the World evangelist throughout the Midwest. In 1920, a group of saints led by Elder J. W. Childs organized a church in Detroit, Michigan. For a brief period, Carson served as the pastor of the small flock. In need of a pastor, the group requested Samuel N. Hancock. He was appointed pastor of what became later known as Bethlehem Temple Church. Carson left Detroit and headed west to Los Angeles in 1922.

He held tent revival meetings teaching and preaching the Apostolic doctrine upon his arrival in Los Angeles. The tent where he initially had his meetings became too small to accommodate the large crowds. Nevertheless, Carson raised enough money to build a church. In 1923, the Apostolic Faith Home Assembly, Inc. was officially incorporated in California. Unfortunately, a few months after the dedication, Carson became seriously ill. Floyd I. Douglas, an early PAW leader from Louisville, Kentucky, succeeded him as pastor.

Dunlap Chenault -1970

Dunlap Chenault was born in Kentucky but later moved to Texas. In 1915, Robert C. Lawson traveled to the Southwest. Following his successful revival in San Antonio, Lawson organized Lincoln Park Church of Christ and appointed Chenault the pastor. The Apostolic doctrine quickly spread in San Antonio and throughout Texas through the preaching of Chenault. The rapid rise of the movement in Texas led to the establishment of the Texas State Council. Lincoln Park operated as the mother church and headquarters for the council.

Chenault rose to prominence in PAW during the influx of black ministers. He was appointed an Executive elder in 1921 and a District Elder in 1924. In 1934, he and a small number of his members split from Lincoln Park and PAW. Chenault organized the East End Church of Christ in San Antonio. Although he no longer served as a PAW member, Chenault remained an influential leader of the Apostolic movement in Texas until he died in 1970.

James I. Clark, Sr. 1901-1972

Educator, pastor, and one of the founding leaders of Bible Way Church of Our Lord Jesus Christ was born in Trinidad, West Indies, where he received his early education. As a young teenager, he came to the United States to live with his aunt and continued schooling at Central High School in Paterson, New Jersey. At nineteen, Clark and a young friend decided to stop in and listen to a church service where Robert C. Lawson was ministering. Unfortunately, his friend left after the service, never to return, but Clark remained and was baptized in Jesus' name. In 1932, Clark organized Bethel Church of Christ in Paterson, New Jersey, serving as pastor for twenty-two years. He later became the pastor of the Strait Gate Church of Mamaroneck, New York, in 1954. During this time, he earned an M.Th. from the American Divinity School.

An ardent Bible student and a promoter of Christian education, in 1940, he developed the Church of Christ Bible Institute and served as its Dean until 1956. In 1957, Clark joined Bible Way Church of Our Lord Jesus Christ, founded by Smallwood E. Williams. Along with George Gary, Odell Lyerly, Carey Robinson, Joseph Powlis, Roy Powlis, and Nathaniel Byrd, he organized Christ Temple in New York City. A few years after, he launched the Bible Way Bible Institute.

Clark was consecrated to the office of bishop in Philadelphia in 1966. As a leader in Bible Way, he served as executive secretary, Diocesan of the New York and Westchester Churches, and Diocesan of the Islands of Jamaica and Trinidad. Clark's desire to develop an accredited Bible school did not come to fruition in the Bible Way organization. He returned to COOLJC and resumed his role as the Dean of the Church of Christ Bible Institute. After suffering a mild heart attack in 1969, Clark turned the leadership of his Harlem congregation over to his son, James I. Clark Jr., and devoted full attention to the institute for the remainder of his life.

Further Reading:
Christ Temple 50th Anniversary Journal. New York, NY: Christ Temple, 2007.

David Collins 1900-1983

Born in Yazoo City, Mississippi, Collins supported his family at twelve after his father's death. In 1923, he relocated to Detroit, Michigan, and worked at Packard Motor Company. Collins encountered the Apostolic message at Clinton Street Greater Bethlehem Temple Church under the leadership of Samuel N. Hancock. Collins was called into ministry a few years later and affiliated with PAW. After his ordination, he assisted Hancock in establishing congregations throughout Michigan in New Haven, Port Huron, Monroe, Jackson, Delray, and Detroit.

Hancock appointed Collins as his Assistant Pastor of Clinton Street in 1952. In 1957, Hancock, Collins, Heardie Leaston, and Willie Lee split with PAW and founded Pentecostal Churches of the Apostolic Faith. Collins succeeded Hancock as pastor of Clinton Street Greater Bethlehem Temple Church after his death in 1963. He served as pastor of the church for seventeen years and emeritus pastor until he died in 1983. Over twenty churches were launched under his leadership.

George Cooke 1885-1974

One of the influential leaders of the Eastern District Council and pastor of the historic Apostolic Faith Assembly in Philadelphia was born in Seaford, Delaware. However, he moved to Philadelphia at an early age. After 1914, early Pentecostal leader Henry Prentiss brought the Apostolic doctrine to South Philadelphia and established the Apostolic Faith Assembly.

Cooke joined Prentiss sometime around 1915 and was called to the ministry soon after. Prentiss left the church for the evangelistic field in 1917. Cooke took over as the pastor, and he joined PAW. Apostolic Faith Assembly held its first convention in 1918, with the featured speakers G. T. Haywood and Robert C. Lawson.

As a PAW leader, Cooke served as the first treasurer and vice-chairman of the Eastern District Council organized by Joseph M. Turpin. He led his congregation for over fifty years. His ministry helped launch several Apostolic churches in Philadelphia, such as Rose of Sharon Church, Pentecostal Bridegroom Temple, and Zion Apostolic Faith Church.

Thomas J. Cox - 1943

The Church of God Apostolic (COGA) founder was a former slave born in Danville, Kentucky. He adopted Holiness in the 1800s and founded the holiness organization Christian Faith Band in Danville in 1897. In 1915, Robert C. Lawson traveled to Kentucky and introduced Cox to Oneness Pentecostalism. That year, he renamed his organization Church of God Apostolic. COGA expanded into Ohio, Virginia, North Carolina, Oklahoma, and West Virginia during his administration. He led the body for forty years until he became too seriously ill to oversee the group. Because of his illness, he turned over the leadership to Eli N. Neal in 1941. Cox died in Danville in 1943.

William Crossley 1908-1981

The leader of the Apostolic movement in western New York was born in Eufaula, Alabama. His family moved to Detroit, Michigan, and attended Greater Bethlehem Temple under the pastorate of Samuel N. Hancock. Crossley served as an Associate Minister but later accepted his first pastorate at Christ Tabernacle in Richmond, Indiana, in 1934. He became the pastor of Emmanuel Tabernacle in Buffalo, New York, in 1939. Within PAW, he served as a District Elder and on the Executive Board as a Director.

In 1959, Crossley founded another church, Emmanuel Temple Apostolic Church. Shortly after, he began a radio broadcast, becoming the first Apostolic minister to preach have a radio broadcast in Buffalo, New York. Next, he was elevated to the bishopric and assigned as Diocesan of the Pacific Northwestern District Council, New York, and Eastern Canada. The diocese's growth led to the formation of the New York State Council and the Canada District Council.

Aletha June Cushinberry 1937-2015

Aletha June Cushinberry was the first woman to be ordained a bishop in Pentecostal Assemblies of the World. She spent her early childhood in Garden City, Kansas, then moved to Topeka. When she relocated to Topeka, she was baptized in the name of Jesus Christ and joined the Apostolic Church of Jesus Christ. Shortly after, Cushinberry accepted the call to preach the gospel. First serving as a Sunday School teacher and in various positions in the church, in 1967, she assumed the pastorate of the Apostolic Church of Jesus Christ.

She rose through the ranks of PAW, breaking barriers for women in ministry. She was the first woman to be elected chairman of the Northwestern District Council, a District Elder, General Secretary, and the first to be named Suffragan bishop. Her ground-breaking achievement came in 2015 when Charles H. Ellis, former presiding bishop of PAW, appointed her a bishop.

In addition to her service as a pastor and leader in PAW, she served on many community boards, including the President of the Minority Housing Corporation of Topeka, the Topeka African American and Pastor's Coalition, and the Topeka Justice Unity Ministry Project. Before her death in 2015, PAW awarded her the "Trailblazer Recognition Award."

Belle Davis 1858-1950

Mother Belle Davis established The Pentecostal Church of the Apostolic Faith, one of the oldest Oneness congregations in the United States. In the 1890s, a small prayer band met in Leavenworth, Kansas. From this group, Davis organized The Pentecostal Church in the early 1900s.

In 1913, Robert C. Lawson brought the Apostolic message to Leavenworth. Davis embraced baptism in the name of Jesus, and she joined Pentecostal Assemblies of the World shortly after. Here, Lawson met his wife, Carrie Fields, an early charter member of the church.

Her son, Herbert Davis, took over as pastor in 1918. Mother Davis led the church for over thirty years. In 1986, the Belle Davis Center opened in honor of its founder. Bishop Kenneth Neal serves as the current pastor of the Pentecostal Church of the Apostolic Faith.

Herbert John Davis 1892-1959
Helen Davis

The early leader of Pentecostal Assemblies of the World was born in Leavenworth, Kansas. He left Leavenworth to pursue a career as a nightclub singer in Los Angeles, California. On his journey back home, Davis was converted to the Pentecostal faith and baptized in Jesus' name in 1918. Belle Davis, his mother and founder of The Pentecostal Church, turned over the church's leadership to him sometime after.

Davis was one of twenty-four black ministers elected as Executive elder in PAW in 1921. He was mainly responsible for the development of the Northwestern District Council, serving as the first Chairman of the council in 1925. Davis served as pastor of The Pentecostal Church, but he also traveled as an evangelist throughout Kansas. He established churches in Missouri, Colorado, Nebraska, Montana, and Oklahoma during his travels. The organization consecrated him to the bishopric in 1954. Davis held that office until he died in 1959.

Raymond Fox Davis 1921-2017
Iolar Burch Davis 1928-2016

The founder and first presiding bishop of Highway Churches of Christ was born in Marion, South Carolina. He was introduced to the apostolic doctrine in 1943 and called into the ministry. Shortly after, he affiliated with Highway Church of Christ (HCCC) under the leadership of James T. Morris. Between 1947 and 1948, Davis traveled back and forth to his hometown, preaching the gospel from house to house. Finally, in 1950, he permanently moved from Philadelphia to Marion, purchasing an old garage building, which once was the first black movie theatre in Marion.

Within HCCC, he served as National Secretary and Overseer of the State of South Carolina. In 1955, Davis established Highway Churches of Christ and was consecrated to the office of bishop in 1958. In addition, Davis pastored Greater Highway Church of Christ in Marion while working as an entrepreneur who operated a radio station, funeral home, beauty shop, and several residential and commercial properties. Davis renamed his group Greater Highway Church of Christ, Incorporated. His organization expanded from South Carolina throughout the eastern region of the United States, Jamaica, West Indies, and Nigeria, Africa.

Riley Marcilous Davis 1894-1997
Mary Sedonia Davis -1980

Riley M. Davis was instrumental in organizing the Brotherhood of Sleeping Car Porters. Born in Americus, Georgia, Davis received his early education in Sumpter County School and later attended Americus Institute Normal High School. He moved to Baltimore in 1916 and worked at Bethlehem Steel. Davis received the baptism of the Holy Spirit at First Apostolic Faith Church in 1923 under the leadership of Joseph M. Turpin. He served as chairman of the Trustee Board, Church Treasurer, and Assistant Superintendent of the National Sunday School of PAW. In 1919, Davis became employed at the Baltimore Ohio Railroad Line as a Pullman Sleeping Car Porter. During his career, he manned B&O; Pullman cars on runs from Baltimore to Chicago and New York.

He worked with A. Phillip Randolph, a leader of the Civil Rights Movement and the American Labor movement. When many black porters were afraid to associate with Randolph, Davis opened his home to the civil rights leader. As a result, Pullman meetings were held at his home. In 1925, Randolph organized and led the Brotherhood of Sleeping Car Porters, the first predominantly black labor union. Davis retired from the B&O railroad in 1962. In 1987, in recognition of his long-standing service, Smallwood E. Williams bestowed the title of "Honorary Bishop" of the Bible Way Church of Our Lord Jesus Christ. Davis died in 1997, at the age of 102.

Nah William Dixon 1932-2014

The founder of the Deaf and Dumb in Liberia, West Africa, was born in River Cess, Liberia. Dixon was called into ministry in 1954. He joined Pentecostal Assemblies of the World in 1958 and served as a District Elder. He was elevated to the office of bishop in 1973 and presided over the 35th Episcopal District. He served as president of the Liberia Council of Churches and founded the Don Stewart Christ Pentecostal Church in Bushrod Island, Monrovia. Dixon rose to prominence during civil unrest in the country. He established Feed My People in New Kru Town, located outside Monrovia. The project provided food for thousands of displaced Liberians. Dixon received the Humanitarian of the Year award for his commitment to peace and charitable work.

Further Reading:
Golder, Morris E. *The Bishops of the Pentecostal Assemblies of the World,* Indianapolis, IN: s.n., 1980.

Robert Oliver Doub 1924-1989

The founding presiding bishop of Shiloh Apostolic Temple Church, Inc. was born in Winston-Salem, North Carolina. At eighteen, he moved to Philadelphia, Pennsylvania, and joined Bright Hope Baptist Church. Doub embraced the Apostolic doctrine and was baptized in the name of Jesus in 1944. J. W. Ardrey ordained him to the ministry in the Apostle Church of Christ in God. Following ordination, Doub preached on the street corners of Philadelphia before establishing Shiloh Apostolic Temple. He was promoted as State supervisor of Pennsylvania after planting congregations throughout Philadelphia.

Doub grew dissatisfied with Aubrey's leadership and disappointed over his denial to be elevated to the office of bishop. The leader split with the parent organization in 1953 and founded Shiloh Apostolic Temple Church, Inc. He used his excellent business acumen and entrepreneurial skills to create employment agencies, daycare centers, and business schools. Doub envisioned a unified apostolic body. In 1987, he established the National Apostolic Fellowship Association and brought together leaders from various Oneness bodies. Doub served as president until his death, in a car accident near Scranton, Pennsylvania, at age sixty-five.

Anna Belle Davis Douglas 1888-1962

Evangelist, preacher, and early leader of the Kentucky State Council was born in Clarksville, Tennessee. She eventually moved to Louisville, Kentucky, and joined the Christian Faith Band, a holiness church founded by Thomas J. Cox. By 1910, the Finished Work doctrine had spread throughout the Pentecostal Movement, and Garfield T. Haywood traveled to Louisville to preach at a meeting held at Christian Faith Band. After hearing Haywood preach a message on the Finished Work of Calvary, a small group that included Douglas, Theresa Coffman, Anna B. Calhoun, and Viola Beeler Breckenridge left the holiness church.

In 1912. Anna Bell's husband, Floyd I. Douglas, became pastor of this group known as the "Louisville Assembly." Shortly after his appointment, the church joined PAW. Anna Bell became an early chartered member of the Kentucky State Council in 1923. She moved with her husband, who took over the pastorate of Apostolic Faith Home Assembly in Los Angeles, California, in 1924. Douglas served as the First Lady of the church for twenty-seven years. Her husband turned over the pastorate to Frank R. Bowdan after becoming ill in 1951.

Douglas traveled as an evangelist throughout the Midwest, East, and West. She accompanied Maggie Bowdan on an evangelistic tour in Sacramento, California, in 1929 before Bowdan's untimely death. Hundreds of people were baptized in the name of Jesus and received the baptism of the Holy Spirit through Douglas' ministry. After the death of her husband, Bishop Floyd I. Douglas, Anna Bell married Bishop Samuel N. Hancock.

Floyd Ignatius Douglas 1887-1951

One of the early black leaders of Pentecostal Assemblies of the World was born in Nelson County, Kentucky. Douglas grew up in the Catholic tradition. As a Catholic, he received his first communion at ten and attended St. Joseph's Catholic School. In 1911, Douglas moved from Nelson County to Louisville, Kentucky. That same year, he left Catholicism after he received the baptism of the Holy Spirit. Douglas received his call to the ministry shortly after his Pentecostal experience.

He became the pastor of a small group split from the Christian Faith Band, a holiness church founded by Thomas J. Cox. With a membership of thirty-five people, Douglas joined PAW. Known as the "Louisville Assembly," the church hosted its first PAW convention in 1915 with G. T. Haywood and A. R. Schooler in attendance.

Douglas had been a credentialed member of PAW as early as 1912. When PAW's leadership was predominately white, Douglas, Haywood, Schooler, and R. C. Lawson were the only black leaders elected to the office of Field Superintendent in 1918. He was elected as Executive elder and appointed chairman of the first district council in Kentucky in 1923. One year later, William A. Carson, founder of the Apostolic Faith Home Assembly in Los

Angeles, California, became seriously ill, and Douglas replaced him as pastor. The church would flourish and grow under his leadership.

PAW appointed Douglas to the office of bishop in 1928. The organization experienced turmoil after the death of Haywood in 1931. Douglas helped reorganize PAW and remained one of its stalwart leaders. He worked closely with Samuel J. Grimes to establish the California State Council in the late 1930s and early 1940s. He also served as Diocesan of the Mountain States District Council (New Mexico and West Texas). Bishop Grimes bestowed Douglas the honorary title of "Senior Bishop" in 1932.

Sydney Alexander Dunn 1921-2017

One of the founding leaders of the Apostolic movement in Jamaica and the United Kingdom was born in St Mary, Jamaica. At seventeen, he encountered the Apostolic doctrine while visiting a church founded by Mother Christine Walsh and her husband, Charles.

In 1940, Dunn was ordained as an elder and appointed pastor of a church in Kilancholly, St. Mary. When the Walshes left the Pentecostal Assemblies of the World in 1945 and founded Shiloh Apostolic Church, Dunn was consecrated as a deputy Bishop and served as General Secretary in their new organization. He emigrated to Great Britain in 1954 as part of the 'Windrush Generation" when many Jamaicans left the island.

One year after he arrived in the United Kingdom, he founded Bethel Church, one of the first Oneness Pentecostal churches in Handsworth, England, and became one of the UK's first black bishops. In 1956, Dunn affiliated with the Church of God in Christ Jesus Apostolic under the leadership of Randolph A. Carr. He was consecrated to the office of bishop along with Monroe A. Saunders and John Watson at the 1957 Holy Convocation.

Dunn joined the United Church of Jesus Christ Apostolic in 1965 and served as Deputy Bishop. By 1966, over twenty churches were birthed from his ministry in England and Jamaica. Dunn later organized Bethel United Church of Jesus Christ Apostolic (UK) in 1991. He served as the presiding bishop of over forty churches in the United Kingdom, the Caribbean, Canada, and Africa.

Further Reading:

A Short History of Bethel United Church of Jesus Christ Apostolic. London, England: Bethel United Church of Jesus Christ Apostolic, 2019.

Johnson, Fitz G. *Born for a Purpose: The Autobiography of Sydney Alexander Dunn.* S.l.: Grosvenor House Publishing Ltd. 2016.

Harry Clay Eggleston 1913-1984

The third presiding bishop of Way of the Cross Church of Christ was born in Henry, Virginia. Eggleston started Shiloh Church in Martinsville, Virginia, in 1943. His church affiliated with the Way of the Cross Church of Christ. Shortly after he joined, membership increased. The rapid growth of his congregation led him to construct a new building that seated over three hundred in 1956. Sometime later, he was consecrated to the office of the bishop.

A community activist in Martinsville, Eggleston, participated in voter registration among African Americans. He often provided transportation to polling stations in his community. He was instrumental in integrating schools and restaurants in Martinsville in the 1960s. Eggleston was also a member of the Voters League and the NAACP. In 1981, he succeeded John Luke Brooks as the third presiding bishop. Leroy H. Cannady, who served as vice presiding bishop, became the organization's fourth presider after Eggleston's death in 1984.

Robert Evans, Jr. 1947-2000

Bishop Robert Evans Jr. was born in Manning, South Carolina. He relocated to Baltimore, Maryland, when he was five years old. Evans was called to the ministry in 1967. He was appointed acting pastor when Overseer Rubin Robinson of Highway Church of Christ became seriously ill. In 1972 when Rubin died, Evans became pastor. After several name changes, Finally, in 1989, Evans changed the name of the church to "Beth-El" Temple to reflect what he understood to be representing God's name. He enrolled in the Baltimore School of the Bible and the Howard University School of Divinity in Washington DC while working first in the Income Tax Division of the State of Maryland.

In 1986 the Highway Churches of Christ consecrated Evans to the office of Bishop. Two years later, he resigned from Highway Churches of Christ to organize the Beth-El Churches of Christ, Inc. In 1994 he was consecrated as an apostle and formed the End-Time World Christian Fellowship Association to provide pastoral leadership for pastors from several Pentecostal organizations. Evans served as the presiding bishop of Beth-El Churches of Christ for eleven years. A noted musician, he recorded several gospel songs including "Old Story," "He's Everything to Me," "Secret Closet," and "Christ is Coming Back."

Isabell Brooks Ford 1920- 1994

Way of the Cross Youth for Christ was organized by Isabell Brooks Ford, the oldest of twelve children born to Henry C., the founder of Way of the Cross, and Willie Shaw Brooks. She studied voice and music at the Howard University School of Fine Arts and Music. In the early 1950's she became overseer of the Young Peoples Union, which she reorganized and named the Youth for Christ. YPU became one of the largest national auxiliaries within the organization.

Ford also worked as a missionary for thirty-seven years, and she traveled to Canada, Ghana, Liberia, and Israel. In addition, she served on numerous auxiliaries such as the Pastor's Aid Club, the Willing Workers' Club, the New Members' Committee, and the Drug and Alcohol Outreach Ministry. In 1990, her brother and former presider of Way of the Cross, Bishop Alphonzo D. Brooks, appointed her "Mother" of the organization.

Lillian Ford 1900-1991

Lillian Ford was the first president of Bible Way Church of Our Lord Jesus Christ Women's Council. Born in Farmville, Virginia, she met and married Reginald R. Ford in 1919. Ford and her husband started ministries in Red Bank, Elizabeth City, and Newark, New Jersey. She was appointed State Mother of the Church of Our Lord Jesus Christ under the leadership of Robert C. Lawson.

A few years after establishing Bible Way World Wide, Smallwood E. Williams organized the National Women's Council in 1959. He appointed Ford the first President. Under her leadership, the Women's Council raised thousands of dollars supporting mission work in West Africa and the West Indies. In addition, she served as District Mother of New Jersey for many years and worked alongside her longtime friend, Bishop Winfield A. Showell, who served as Diocesan leader of New Jersey.

John Wesley Garlington, Jr. 1937-1986

Pastor and social justice activist in Oregon during the late 1970s and early 1980s. He was born in Buffalo, New York; his father, John W. Garlington, Sr., founded the Church of God and True Holiness. He served as presiding bishop of that organization from 1968 until 1975. Garlington moved his family to Portland in 1976 to be the pastor of the interracial Maranatha Church in Northeast Portland.

During his tenure, Garlington involved Maranatha in funding Head Start programs and the establishment of Martin Luther King Jr.'s birthday as a state holiday. In addition, the church hosted activists including Jesse Jackson and South African Bishop Desmond Tutu. Garlington also became a leader and spokesman for social justice issues such as education, employment, police-community relations, and ministries to the poor, hungry, and the homeless.

He was president of the Albina Ministerial Alliance and the Police Internal Investigations Auditing Committee chairman to monitor the Portland Police Bureau's handling of public complaints. Before his death, he was installed as the first African American president of Ecumenical Ministries of Oregon. Garlington and his wife, Yvonne, were killed in a tragic car accident while traveling in Florida in 1986. Portland officials renamed the Cascadia's Center, a mental health clinic and social services center, the Cascadia's Garlington Center in honor of Garlington and his wife in 1989.

John Wesley Garlington, Sr. 1884-1943

The founder and first presiding bishop of the Church of God and True Holiness was born in Lawrence, South Carolina; in the early 1900s, he migrated to New York City. By the 1920's he relocated to Buffalo, New York, and established The Churches of God and True Holiness in 1927. The headquarters for the organization was first located in Buffalo. From that city, congregations started in parts of New York, Virginia, North Carolina, Ohio, and South Carolina.

Garlington led this organization until his death in 1943. He died at fifty-five years old, leaving behind a wife and seven children. His son, pastor, and social activist John Wesley Garlington, Jr. served a term as presiding bishop of the organization. Joseph Garlington, megachurch pastor, musician, and noted conference speaker, was another one of his prominent sons.

William Gerald 1918-2012

The first General Secretary of Bible Way Church of Our Lord Jesus Christ was born in Fitzgerald, Georgia. He moved to Washington, DC, when he was five years old. Gerald graduated from Cardozo High School in 1938. Upon graduation, he attended Cortez Peters Business College and Howard University. He received a Doctorate Degree in Theology in 1981 and an honorary Doctor of Divinity in 1988. Ordained to the eldership in 1955, Gerald served as the Radio Narrator for the Bible Way Broadcast on WOOK every Sunday morning for twenty years.

He was one of two black radio announcers in DC and a former member of the American Federation of Television and Radio Artists. Gerald served as editor of the Bible Way News Voice newspaper for fifteen years. In addition, he authored ten books, including *A Panoramic View of the Basics of Holiness*, *Christian Psychiatry*, *Coping with and Overcoming Today's Problems*, *Divine Basics and Concepts*, and *A Concise Resume of Biblical Expositions*. In 1963, Gerald started his ministry, Lighthouse Church in Annapolis, Maryland. Sometime later, he established a Sunday radio broadcast at WANN that spanned over twenty-five years. Gerald also organized local congregations in Seat Pleasant, Shady Side, Harwood, and Mayo, Maryland.

Morris Ellis Golder 1913-2000

Historian, Preacher, Theologian, and Pastor Golder was born in Indianapolis, Indiana. His parents were converted at the historic Christ Temple under the pastorate of Bishop G. T. Haywood. Golder aspired to become a jazz bandleader as a young man, but his life changed in 1930. He was saved and baptized in Jesus' name at Christ Temple. Golder received his call to the ministry following his conversion. He learned his methodology of teaching the scriptures under the tutelage of Haywood. In 1931, Haywood died, and Robert F. Tobin succeeded him as pastor of Christ Temple. Tobin's fiery preaching style influenced Golder, who later became one of the great Apostolic orators.

In 1935, he was appointed pastor of Bethesda Temple in St. Louis, Missouri. Bethesda Temple attracted both white and black believers. Thus, it became the first racially integrated church in St. Louis. Golder's mentor Tobin died unexpectedly in 1947. In 1948, he moved back to Indianapolis and took over as pastor of Christ Temple. He remained at Christ Temple until 1953. Golder organized another work in Indianapolis, Grace Apostolic Church, and pastored the church for forty-seven years.

Golder received a Master of Arts degree from Butler University and an honorary doctorate from Aenon Bible College.

In 1933, Samuel J. Grimes appointed Golder, the first historian of the National Pentecostal Young People's Union. As a PAW historian, Golder documented the history of PAW in his seminal work, "*History of the Pentecostal Assemblies of the World.*" He also authored *The Life and Works of Bishop Garfield Thomas Haywood (1880-1931) and the Bishops of the Pentecostal Assemblies of the World, Inc.* He was the third Editor of The Christian Outlook (1949 – 1953), following Haywood and Grimes. Golder was consecrated Bishop in 1972. He also served as Treasurer and Vice President of the board of directors at Aenon Bible College.

Further Reading:
Gary W. Garrett and Nathaniel A. Urshan. *The Life and Times of Bishop Morris E. Golder.* Eureka, IL: Apostolic Christian, 2000.

Benjamin J. Goode (B.J.) 1895-

Founding publisher of the *"The Apostolic Voice."* Born in South Carolina, Goode migrated to Columbus, Ohio. He joined the Church of Christ of the Apostolic Faith and Pentecostal Assemblies of the World. Goode served as the assistant pastor under the leadership of Karl F. Smith for several years. After 1941, Goode relocated to Detroit, Michigan, and founded Bethel Apostolic Faith Church. In the 1950s, he began publishing the independent monthly periodical "The Apostolic Voice." The publication was circulated throughout the United States.

Randolph Goodwin 1917-2000

The founder and first presiding bishop of the Holy Temple Church of the Lord Jesus Christ of the Apostolic Faith was born in Columbia, South Carolina. He migrated to the Bronx, New York, and worked as a barber. Called to preach in 1947, he established a small congregation in the back of his barbershop shortly after. For several years, Goodwin worked under Sherrod C. Johnson, founder of the Church of the Lord Jesus Christ.

When Johnson died in 1961 and former vice president, S. McDowell Shelton, took over the organization, Goodwin pulled out of the body and used his Bronx congregation to launch his new organization. Goodwin led Holy Temple for nearly forty years until he died in 2002. Under his leadership, the organization expanded along the East Coast and in the Caribbean, West Africa, and the Philippines. Goodwin wrote over twenty-five tracts defending the Oneness/apostolic doctrine. He also reproduced several tracts written by his mentor, Bishop Sherrod C. Johnson.

Simon Tenyen Grant 1904-

The African leader was born in Simon Cape Palmas, Liberia. Grant embraced the Christian faith in 1927. He was called into the ministry in 1931 and joined Pentecostal Assemblies of the World shortly after. Grant established the First Pentecostal Church in Sierra Leone and served as pastor for forty-one years. He was elevated to the bishopric in 1970 and appointed Chairman of the Sierra District Council. Sometime after, Grant presided over the 34th Episcopal District for nine years. He was instrumental in the development of the Apostolic movement in Liberia.

Ralph E. Green 1935-2018
Shirley M. Green 1939-2020

The founder and first presiding bishop of the Free Gospel Church of the Apostles' Doctrine was born in Nelson County, Virginia. The former Golden Globe boxer served in the United States Army. Then, he joined the Way of the Cross Church of Christ. Green left WOTCC and established the Free Gospel Deliverance Temple in Washington, DC. A few years after founding Free Gospel, he began a radio ministry on WUST in DC. Soon after, Green developed a progressive prison outreach ministry that included the publication of a monthly periodical, *From Prison to Praise*.

In 1962, Green organized the Free Gospel Church of the Apostles' Doctrine. He also established the Open Bible Institute for Christian Apologetics and the Free Gospel Christian Academy. His organization has congregations throughout the District of Columbia, Maryland, North Carolina, Virginia, Africa, and the Philippines. In addition, Green affiliated with and served as Vice-President of the National Apostolic Fellowship Association, Inc., founded by Robert O. Doub in 1987. His wife, Dr. Shirley Green, served as pastor of Free Gospel Churches of the Apostles' Doctrine after his death in 2018.

Martin Rawleigh Gregory 1885-1960

The founder of Emmanuel Tabernacle Baptist Church Apostolic was born in Virginia. Gregory preached his first sermon at the age of seventeen. In 1903, he was ordained as a Baptist minister. He received his education at Colgate University in Rochester, New York, studying law and medicine. In 1914, Gregory moved to Columbus, Ohio, and sometime in 1916, he encountered the Apostolic message through the ministry of Robert C. Lawson. His acceptance of Oneness Pentecostalism caused him to break with the Baptist church.

Gregory and two former Baptists, Lela Grant and Bessie Dockett, established Emmanuel Tabernacle Baptist Church in 1916. Grant and Dockett were the first women ordained to the office of bishop in the Apostolic movement. ETBC expanded its initial growth from Ohio into Virginia, North Carolina, and West Virginia, where Gregory established Apostolic Temple. However, in 1930, the church he founded in Gary experienced a schism, and most of its members affiliated with PAW.

Gregory encountered Mother Lulu Phillips, one of the founding leaders of the Glorious Church of God in Christ, while pastoring in West Virginia in 1919. She invited him to speak at her church in Huntington concerning baptism in Jesus' name and the

Oneness of God. Phillips and fifty congregation members were baptized after hearing Gregory's teaching. Following her baptism, her organization adopted the Apostolic doctrine. Gregory died in 1960. ETBC currently has thirty churches in Ohio, Florida, Maryland, West Virginia, Virginia, and North Carolina.

Samuel Joshua Grimes 1884-1967

Missionary and the second presiding bishop of Pentecostal Assemblies of the World Liberia, West Africa, was born in Barbados, British West Indies. Grimes grew up in the Wesleyan Methodist Church and expressed a desire to preach at a young age. His family moved to the United States in 1905. He acknowledged his call to preach in 1911 while living in Philadelphia, Pennsylvania. Grimes enrolled at the National Bible Institute of Philadelphia (now Cairn University) and graduated from the National Bible Institute of New York (later Shelton College) in 1917.

He visited the Apostolic Faith Assembly, where he experienced the baptism of the Holy Spirit under the ministry of Henry Prentiss in Philadelphia. During his last year in school, he began an extensive evangelistic tour. During that period, he heard Pentecostal leader G. T. Haywood preach, accepted the Apostolic doctrine, and was baptized in Jesus' name in Cleveland, Ohio. In 1920, Grimes traveled to Liberia, West Africa, as a PAW missionary. He spent four years in the country and returned to America in 1924. Following one of his missionary trips to Liberia, he and his wife, Kathleen, sponsored Ellen Moore-Hopkins' education in the United States. The Grimes were helpful in

Hopkins establishing the Samuel K. Grimes Child Welfare Center in Kakata, Liberia.

Upon his return from the mission field, he joined the Eastern District Council and served as the longtime editor of *The Christian Outlook*, the official publication of PAW. After the death of Haywood in 1931, Grimes attended the meeting to re-organize PAW. Still, after a failed merger with Pentecostal Assemblies of Jesus Christ, he was unanimously elected as the presiding bishop, the post he held for thirty-five years.

Grimes organized several churches throughout the east coast, yet he never pastored a local church. He established thirteen district councils from Maine to Florida. Under his leadership, the National Pentecostal Young People's Union, the Women's Federation, and the Aenon Bible College were established. Grimes served as presider from 1932 to 1967, and his leadership stabilized PAW during a period of turmoil.

Sobrina Kathleen Grimes (S.K.) 1881-1960

Missionary, composer, musician, and the first wife of Samuel J. Grimes, the second presider of Pentecostal Assemblies of the World, was born in Canada but migrated to New York in 1910. Kathleen and her husband served as missionaries in Liberia, West Africa, from 1920 to 1924. Unfortunately, she contracted malaria in Liberia, an illness that afflicted her for the remainder of her life.

After returning to America, Kathleen and Samuel settled in New York and ministered in evangelistic campaigns across the United States and Canada. Grimes, an accomplished musician, and songwriter penned her first hymn, "Since the Comforter Came." in 1909, a few years after the Azusa Street Revival. The song was a testimony to her personal Pentecostal experience of Spirit baptism. She published an eight-song collection entitled *Echoes of Zion* in 1924. Her most famous song, "The Great I Am," was included in the Bridegroom Songs collection published by PAW.

In 1932, she became the first lady of PAW after her husband was elected to the office of presiding bishop. As the first lady, Grimes was instrumental in organizing PAW's women's auxiliary. She and her husband also sponsored the education of Ellen Moore Hopkins, a nursing student from Liberia, West Africa. Hopkins established the Samuel Grimes Maternity and Welfare Center in Kakola, Liberia. The center assisted hundreds of orphans and trained hundreds of nurses in Liberia. Grimes also served as a leader of the PAW's Virginia State Council until her death in 1960.

Further Reading:
Sims, Jane A. *Telling Our Story: The Role and Contributions of Women, Particularly Women of Color, in the Formation of the Pentecostal/Holiness Movement and the Pentecostal Assemblies of the World.* 2002.

Isaiah Warren Hamiter 1919-1985

The Second presiding bishop of the Original Glorious Church of God in Christ was born in Cincinnati, Ohio. By the early 1930s, the family had relocated to Huntington, West Virginia, joining the Glorious Church of God in Christ. Hamiter pastored Glorious Faith Tabernacle in Oberlin, Ohio, from 1947 to 1949. Later that year, the organization ordained him to the office of bishop and appointed him overseer of West Virginia. Hamiter moved to Columbus, Ohio, where he led a storefront congregation.

The small church gradually grew to purchase a large convention center for the Glorious Church organization. When Sidney Coy Bass defied the Glorious Church of God's charter in 1952 to marry a divorced woman, he left that organization to start the Original Glorious Church of God in Christ. W. O. Howard served as the first presiding bishop of the newly formed body until 1972. Hamiter took over after the retirement of Howard. During his tenure, new mission programs developed in Haiti, Jamaica, and India. He presided over Original Glorious Church for thirteen years.

Samuel Nathan Hancock 1883-1963

The influential leader and founder of the Apostolic Faith Pentecostal Churches was born in Adair, Kentucky. Hancock's family moved to Indianapolis, Indiana, in 1888 when he was five. At age thirteen, he dropped out of seventh grade to work on the railroad to help support his family. In 1912, Hancock attended Apostolic Faith Assembly led by G. T. Haywood. He received Spirit baptism and began preaching on the Indianapolis streets in 1914. By 1915, the Oneness Pentecostal revival spread to the Midwest. That same year, Hancock and 465 members of Christ Temple were baptized in Jesus' name by the Pentecostal leader, Glen A. Cook. A few years later, he was ordained to the eldership and served as Haywood's assistant pastor.

He moved to Detroit, Michigan, in 1921 to pastor Bethlehem Temple, a church that grew to more than 3,000 parishioners under his leadership. During his tenure as pastor, Hancock developed a soup kitchen that fed the poor throughout the Great Depression, a boys' workshop that taught carpentry and trade skills, a church-owned supermarket, a church farm, and a girls' home.

In 1927, Hancock was elevated to the office of bishop and served as Diocesan over Illinois, Nebraska, Wyoming, and Iowa.

After Haywood died in 1931, the predominantly white Pentecostal Ministerial Alliance leaders approached PAW about a merger, which transpired quickly with the two organizations combining to form the Pentecostal Assemblies of Jesus Christ. Subsequently, when that tentative merger failed, the PAW restored its charter under the leadership of Samuel J. Grimes. Hancock and several black presbyters remained in PAJC.

In 1938, however, many of the Blacks returned to PAW after racial tension arose in the new body. By 1940 at the height of his ministry within the PAW, Hancock was accused of teaching that Jesus Christ was only the son of God, not God Himself. After being vindicated by a council of leaders in 1943, he was appointed to the Board of Directors of at, Aenon Bible School.

In 1952, Hancock challenged Grimes's position as presiding bishop. Grimes defeated him in a run-off election at the 27th General Assembly held at the First Apostolic Faith Church in Baltimore, Maryland. As a result, Hancock left PAW and formed the Pentecostal Churches of the Apostolic Faith with PAW ministers, David Collins, Heardie Leaston, and Willie Lee in 1957. He served as presiding bishop of PCAF until his death at seventy-nine. Hancock left an organization of nearly six hundred churches throughout the United States, Africa, and the Caribbean.

Gladstone Theophilus Harewood 1898-1990

Gladstone T. Harewood, the prolific hymnist and songwriter was born in St. Lucia, West Indies, in 1898. His father served in the British colonial army, and his mother died when he was an infant. The Harewood family immigrated to the United States in 1908, and Gladstone lived with his uncle in Chicago. His brother, Richard Harewood, would become the first black to win statewide public office in Illinois. He later served as a judge in the Circuit Court of Cook County. Harewood joined the Apostolic Faith Church, founded by A. R. Schooler in Chicago, and served as assistant pastor with John S. Holly in 1924. He took over the leadership of a small mission once led by Theodore Sherriff in 1928 and served as a member of the Illinois State Council.

Harewood wrote over a hundred songs. Many hymns were credited to G. T. Haywood, songwriter and the first presiding bishop of PAW. His most famous songs include "The Blood Prevails," "I Love Jesus Best of All," "Draw Me, Dear Jesus," and "Now I'm Saved." Harewood lived in several Midwestern states before he settled in Los Angeles. He pastored and led a congregation there until 1985.

Thoro Harris 1874-1955

One of the greatest Pentecostal songwriters who wrote over a thousand hymns. The son of Joseph and Elizabeth Harris, born in Washington, DC. His father was African American, and his mother was German. Some accounts claim that Harris was "Caucasian" or "passed as white." However, most major musical publications list Harris's ethnicity as (Black)African American. In 1902 after attending college in Battle Creek, Michigan, he lived in Boston and Chicago. He produced his first hymnal, which contained many of his compositions. Sometime after 1914, Harris embraced Oneness Pentecostalism and was baptized in the name of Jesus by Oneness Veteran Frank Ewart. After his conversion to the movement, Harris co-wrote several hymns with A. R. Schooler, a one-time leader in the Pentecostal Assemblies of the World.

In 1920 Harris went to Los Angeles to work with Aimee Semple McPherson to compile the Pentecostal Revivalist, a 241-selection hymnal. He then moved to Chicago, Illinois, at the invitation of popular singing evangelist and hymnal publisher Peter Bilhorn. For a time, Harris pastored Lake Street Mission in that city. Though he was never Baptist, in 1925, he edited The New Hymnal, the first collection of Swedish-American Baptist hymns published in English (and containing thirty-nine of his songs). In addition to composing hymns, Harris compiled several hymnals. He was one of the first musicians to produce exclusively Pentecostal hymnals: The Blessed Hope (1910), Jesus Is Coming Soon (1914), Songs of His Coming (1919), and Songs We Love (1921). The multi-talented Harris wrote both texts and tunes and sometimes arranged other composers' melodies.

Harris worked with several famous preachers throughout his life, including the renowned Billy Sunday and Dwight L. Moody. His most famous composition, "All That Thrills My Soul is Jesus," is popular among Oneness and Trinitarian Pentecostals. His hymn, "He's Coming Soon," was adapted to the tune of the famous Hawaiian "Aloha Oe" by Queen Liliuokalani. Harris died at age eighty-one in Eureka Springs.

Further Readings:

Blumhofer, Edith L. *Pentecost in My Soul: Explorations in the Meaning of Pentecostal Experience in the Early Assemblies of God*. Springfield, MO: Gospel Publishing, 1989.

Wallace, Mary H. *Profiles of Pentecostal Preachers*. Hazelwood, MO: Word Aflame, 1983.

Garfield Thomas Haywood 1880-1931

Theologian, songwriter, preacher, mentor, and first presiding bishop of Pentecostal Assemblies was born in Greencastle, Indiana. His family attended St. Paul Baptist Church during his youth, but Haywood was active in a local Methodist congregation, serving as Sunday school superintendent. He met and married his wife, Ida Howard, in 1902 and spent his early years employed as a writer and cartoonist for the African American newspaper, *Indianapolis Freeman*. His cartoons were commentaries on racism, injustice, and discrimination in America.

Pentecostalism reached Indianapolis mainly due to the evangelistic work of Glen A. Cook, who was an early participant of the Azusa Street Revival led by William J. Seymour. Cook held several successful revivals in Indianapolis in 1907. While visiting Los Angeles, California, Cook met Henry Prentiss, an African American who attended the Azusa Street Revival. He heard about a small group of Spirit-filled believers needing a pastor and sent Prentiss to Indianapolis to pastor the small mission.

At the request of his friend, Oddous Barber, Haywood visited Apostolic Faith Assembly and heard Prentiss preach about the baptism of the Holy Spirit. He and his wife received the baptism of the Holy Spirit, and shortly after, he was ordained to the ministry. Haywood and Barber worked alongside Prentiss after his ordination in 1908. For reasons unknown, in 1909, Prentiss left the church and turned the leadership over to Haywood. Apostolic Faith flourished under his leadership. The membership had grown from thirteen to fifty members within a few years. Later renamed Christ Temple, the church became one of the largest interracial Pentecostal congregations in the United States.

Haywood joined Pentecostal Assemblies of the World in 1911 and worked closely with J. J. Frazee, the first General Superintendent of the organization. When he joined PAW, Haywood had established himself as a well-known Pentecostal preacher and publisher of the popular newsletter "Voice in the Wilderness." In 1915, Cook introduced the Oneness doctrine to Haywood. He did not initially respond to Cook's message but prayerfully waited several days before he embraced the message. Finally, sometime in March 1915, he was baptized in the name of Jesus.

Haywood was one of four blacks who served as Field Superintendent in PAW in 1918; the others included F. I. Douglas, Robert C. Lawson, and A. R. Schooler. He was elected General Secretary of the organization in 1919. His prominence and leadership drew many black ministers to PAW. Often characterized as someone "devoid of racial prejudice," in his quiet manner, Haywood pushed for the inclusion of blacks in the leadership during a time when PAW's leadership was predominately white.

By 1924, Racial tensions arose in PAW after blacks moved into positions of authority. A proposal to divide the organization into a white and black branch failed. Haywood's plea for unity was ignored, and most white members left the organization in 1924. In 1925, PAW adopted an episcopal form of government, and Haywood was elected the first presiding bishop. From 1925 to 1931, he led a predominately black organization. During his tenure, PAW grew to over 2,000 churches and 250,000 members.

Haywood was a theologian, apologist, composer, and hymnist. He and Oneness leaders Frank Ewart and Andrew David Urshan formulated most of the early Oneness theology. His writings include *"The Victim of the Flaming Sword" and "The Finest of Wheat."* In addition, Haywood's hymns such as Jesus, the Son of God," "I See a Crimson Stream of Blood," Thank God for the Blood, Baptized into the Body, and "Do All in Jesus' Name" appealed to Oneness and Trinitarian Pentecostals.

Haywood led PAW at the height of the rise of the Apostolic movement. His leadership was pivotal to the spread of the movement throughout the Midwest, South, West, and Eastern regions of America. As a testimony to his influence, in 1980, he city of Indianapolis renamed Fall Creek Drive, where Christ Temple is located, the "Bishop Garfield T. Haywood Memorial Way.

Further Reading:

Golder, Morris E. *The Life and Works of Bishop Garfield Thomas Haywood (1880-1931)*. Indianapolis, IN: s.n., 1977.

Haywood, G T, and Paul D. Dugas. *The Life and Writings of Elder G. T. Haywood*. Portland, OR: Apostolic Book Publishers, 1968.

Ida Hancock Haywood 1884-1954

Ida Haywood Hancock was born in 1884 in Owensboro, Kentucky. She moved to Indianapolis, Indiana, sometime in the 1900s. At eighteen, she met and married Garfield T. Haywood in 1902. Ida received the baptism of the Holy Spirit at the Apostolic Faith Assembly under the ministry of Henry Prentiss in 1907. A few years later, she became the first lady of the Apostolic Faith Assembly, later renamed Christ Temple, after her husband took over the leadership.

In 1925, Garfield was elected the first presiding bishop of PAW. Ida had the distinction of serving as the "first" first lady of the organization. She traveled extensively with her husband throughout the United States, Canada, Europe, the Caribbean, and Israel during his tenure from 1925 to 1931. Ida was instrumental in the initial development of PAW's Women's Department. She served as the first treasurer of the National Women's Auxiliary. After the death of Haywood, she married Samuel N. Hancock in 1939 and lived in Detroit, Michigan until her death in 1954.

John Silas Holly 1901-1979

An influential Pentecostal Assemblies of the World leader, who officiated the consecration of the five founding bishops of Bible Way Church of Our Lord Jesus Christ, was born in Monroe, Louisiana. Holly moved to Chicago, Illinois, in 1919 at the age of eighteen. He joined the Apostolic Faith Church led by A. R. Schooler and received his call to the ministry in 1921. In 1931, when Schooler resigned as pastor G. T. Haywood appointed Holly to fill the vacancy he held for forty-eight years.

Holly was elevated to the office of bishop in 1953 and presided over the 8th Episcopal District of Illinois for twenty-six years. In 1957 he consecrated the original five bishops, led by Smallwood E. Williams, John S. Beane, Winfield A. Showell, McKinley Williams, and Joseph Moore of new the Bible Way Church of Our Lord Jesus Christ in Washington DC. In 1963, Williams established the Apostolic Inter-Organizational Fellowship Conference. Holly served as treasurer and Vice-Chairman of the fellowship for nine years. When Holly died in Chicago at seventy-nine, he had been a PAW member for sixty-six years.

Aaron James Holmes -1958
Pearl Julia Holmes -1965

Aaron and Pearl Holmes were missionaries in Liberia, West Africa, for over forty years. Born in Little Rock, Arkansas, Pearl made her first missionary journey to Africa in 1896. Aaron, a sharecropper from Florida, arrived in Liberia in 1914. After their spouses died, they met and married in 1916. The couple embraced Oneness Pentecostalism and affiliated with the Pentecostal Ministerial Alliance, later renamed Pentecostal Church Incorporated in 1924, PCI merged with Pentecostal Assemblies of Jesus Christ. The Holmes established the Zoradee Pentecostal Mission and School, which still exists as part of UPCI foreign mission work in Liberia. Aaron died at the age of seventy-three in 1958. He served as a missionary for forty-four years. Pearl retired and returned to America in 1961. She had served as a missionary to Africa for sixty-three years.

Further Reading:
Wallace, Mary H. *Profiles of Pentecostal Missionaries*. Hazelwood, MO: Word Aflame Press, 1986.

Ellen Moore Hopkins 1921-2000

The devoted missionary established the Samuel K. Grimes Child Welfare Center in Liberia, West Africa. Born in Talla, Liberia, West Africa, Hopkins wrote Samuel J. Grimes, the second presiding bishop of Pentecostal Assemblies of the World, requesting assistance with her education. Grimes and his wife Kathleen sponsored her, and she attended the Lincoln School of Nursing in Bronx, New York. Hopkins continued her education at the Maternity Center in New York and became a licensed midwife. She earned a bachelor's degree from the Public Health Medical College in Richmond, Virginia, and a master's degree from American University in Washington, DC.

In 1946, she returned to Africa and established the Samuel K. Grimes Child Welfare Center in Kakata, Liberia. The center housed a youth worship center, a hospital for women, children, infants, and a clinic. Her center cared for thousands of babies and trained 136 nurses who served throughout Liberia. Hopkins returned to the United States during civil unrest In her native country. She continued to promote public health for women and children until her death in 2000 in Zanesville, Ohio.

W. O. Howard

W. O. Howard founder of the Original Glorious Church of God in Christ of the Apostolic Faith. Before 1952, Howard served as State Overseer of Ohio and on the Board of Elders under the leadership of presiding bishop Sidney Coy Bass. When Bass defied church doctrine in his decision to marry a divorced woman, Howard and several other GCOGIC bishops reorganized under the leadership of Howard and took the name Original Glorious Church of God in Christ Apostolic Faith. During Howard's tenure at its head, fifteen congregations were added to OGCOGIC. Howard led the group until 1972 when he retired because of poor health.

Lenist J. Hunter 1914-1991

The founder and first presiding bishop of the Church in the Lord Jesus Christ of the Apostolic Faith was born in Darlington, South Carolina. He acknowledged his call into the ministry at the age of twenty-six. Years after his call to preach, he migrated to Philadelphia, Pennsylvania, and preached his first sermon at Bishop Sherrod C. Johnson's Church in Philadelphia in 1943. In 1946, Johnson, who founded the Church of the Lord Jesus Christ, sent Hunter back to his hometown to organize a congregation in that region of the South.

Upon his return, he began a small fellowship in a storefront building. A few years after, his Church moved and held worship services in a tent for over a year. Hunter expanded his ministry to include a radio broadcast in 1956 that continues on several stations through the Faith Radio Network. Finally, he split with Johnson and formed a Church in the Lord Jesus Christ of the Apostolic Faith. He established congregations throughout South Carolina, Alabama, Washington, DC, Pennsylvania, New York, Ohio, and Virginia and led his organization until seventy-seven.

Maurice H. Hutner 1912-1962
Ruth Hutner

Apostle Maurice H. Hutner was born in Birmingham, Alabama. He led a Church of Our Lord Jesus Christ congregation in New Rochelle, New York. His wife, Ruth, served as a missionary in COOLJC. After, Robert C. Lawson's death in 1961, COOLJC elected Hutner to the three-man board of Apostles with William L. Bonner and Hubert L Spencer. The board elected Spencer as presiding bishop of the organization. Hutner died at the age of fifty, one year after the election.

Lulu Jackson 1907-1994

Influential women's leader, preacher, and pastor was born in Cobbs, Georgia. She received the baptism of the Holy Spirit at Emmanuel Church of Christ, founded by Walter Griffin in Newark, New Jersey, in 1920. Jackson moved to Waterbury, Connecticut, and founded Pentecostal Assembly Church, a small storefront, in 1937. Her church outgrew the storefront building and moved into a new facility in 1951. Ten years later, Jackson began airing weekly radio broadcasts on WATR in Westbury that expanded her influence, drawing significant numbers to her church.

She established eight churches and served as 1st and 2nd vice president of the Connecticut District Council. She was also president of the International Missionary and Women's Auxiliary. In addition, Jackson was the first woman to be elected to PAW's Board of Bishops as Lay Director of the Northeast district. Besides being a pastor, and preacher, Jackson penned gospel songs, "I'm So Glad I Got the Holy Ghost," "Thank You, Jesus," and "When My Work on Earth is Through."

Norma Sylvester Jackson 1913-2005

Educator, Administrator, and Dean of Aenon Bible College, West Coast branch, was born in Brooklyn, New York. Jackson was educated in New York public schools. She attended King's Chapel in Harlem, New York. There she was baptized in the name of Jesus and received the baptism of the Holy Spirit.

Jackson felt called to attend Aenon Bible College. At the age of twenty-six, a single mother with two children, she moved to Columbus, Ohio. She attended the Church of Christ of the Apostolic Faith under the leadership of Karl F. Smith, who became her mentor. Jackson graduated from Aenon with a degree in Religious Education. She was bestowed with an Honorary Doctor of Divinity in 1994.

In 1967, she moved to Los Angeles and joined Apostolic Faith Home Assembly led by Frank R. Bowdan. Jackson traveled as a national evangelist in PAW during the time. In 1972, Bowdan established Aenon School of Theology and Bible College, a west coast campus. He appointed Jackson Dean of the school in 1973. She served as dean and in various capacities at the school for thirty-two years.

James Archie Johnson 1924-2015

The former presiding bishop of Pentecostal Assemblies of the World and prominent pastor in St. Louis, Missouri, was born in Flint, Michigan. He was saved under Frank R. Bowdan in 1939 and called into the ministry in 1943. Johnson left Flint in 1950 and assumed the pastorate of Bethesda Temple Church of the Apostolic Faith in St. Louis, Missouri. Bethesda Temple initially began in 1935 with a small group of believers. The group joined PAW, and Morris Golder was assigned the pastorate. Under Johnson's leadership, the church membership reached over 1,000 people, and it outgrew three buildings.

Johnson received his Bachelor of Arts degree in Christian Education and a Master of Theology. He holds Doctoral degrees in Christian Education and Philosophy from the International Apostolic College of Grace & Truth in Dayton, Ohio, and a Doctor of Divinity from Aenon Bible College in Indianapolis, Indiana. He authored several books, *Enduring the Night, Jesus Christ, With Us God, Theology of the Cross,* and *The Name of Jesus Christ as Immanuel*.

In 1961, Johnson was named General Executive of PAW. He was elevated to the office of bishop in 1968 and elected to PAW's board of Directors. In addition, Johnson served as Vice-chairmen of the Mid-Western District Council. He was appointed the sixth presiding bishop of PAW in 1986 and oversaw the organization until 1992.

Lymus Leewood Johnson 1922-2012

The National Evangelist and the founder of the Evangelistic Churches of Christ of the Apostolic Faith was born in Coster (Calvert County), Maryland. Johnson later relocated to Asbury Park, New Jersey. He received the baptism of the Holy Spirit at the age of nine and preached his first sermon at St. Johns Methodist Church. After moving to Trenton, New Jersey, he met and married his wife Ruth Robinson, who attended Sherrod C. Johnson's church. Lymus traveled throughout the United States as a revivalist during the 1930s and 1940s. His revival meetings often lasted for weeks or sometimes months. Once, he preached at Refuge Temple in New York while Robert C. Lawson visited Africa. Over 100 people were baptized in Jesus' name, and seventy-five were filled with the Holy Spirit at the month-long revival.

In 1956, Lawson appointed Johnson to the office of National Evangelist and Chair of the National Evangelistic Board. As the nationalist evangelist for COOLJC, Johnson traveled the country, preaching the gospel. He left the COOLJC in 1974 to organize the Evangelistic Churches of Christ in Corona, New York. The congregation grew and was later located in Jackson Heights, New York, now the headquarters. In 1982, after the death of McKinley Williams, one of the founding leaders of Bible Way Church of Our

Lord Jesus Christ, Johnson took over as pastor of the Refuge Church of Christ in Philadelphia, Pennsylvania. He went on to take his gospel to the world by radio broadcast.

Further Reading:
Walters, Steve B. *A Shepherd's Journey: The Life Story of Apostle Lymus L. Johnson.* n.p.: Steve Walters Ministries, 2002.

Margaret Giles Johnson

Church of Our Lord Jesus Christ foreign missionary to Liberia, West Africa. At seven, Margret told her mother she would travel to Africa as a missionary. Several years later, she received the baptism of the Holy Spirit under the leadership of Robert C. Lawson at Refuge Temple in New York City in 1938. Sometime after, Johnson approached Lawson about her desire to go on the mission field in Africa. With Lawson's s blessings, she journeyed to Liberia during the height of World War II in 1944.

She spent three weeks in Monrovia and later worked with missionaries Aaron and Pearl Holmes, who founded the United Pentecostal Church International Zoradee Pentecostal Mission. Johnson completed her work with the Holmes and traveled to the town of Bola, where over three hundred people were converted and received the baptism of the Holy Spirit. In 1946, she established the Zuie Refuge Mission, which housed a chapel, school, boys and girls' dormitory, teacher's house, and a maternity clinic for women.

In 1953, Johnson became seriously ill and was carried to the hospital in a hammock by African natives. She returned to New York City after being hospitalized for two months in Monrovia. Johnson continued to support Zuie Refuge Mission and foreign missions work throughout Africa. She served as a COOLJC missionary for nine years.

Further Reading:
Casselberry, Judith. *The Labor of Faith: Gender and Power In Black Apostolic Pentecostalism.* Durham : Duke University Press,2017.

DuPree, Sherry Sherrod. *Biographical Dictionary of African American Holiness-Pentecostal 1880-1990.* Washington: Mid-Atlanta Regional, 1989.

Johnson, Margaret G. *My Call to Africa.* n.p.: n.p., n.d.

Sherrod Charlotte Johnson (S.C.) 1897-1961

Sherrod C. Johnson was the founder of the Church of the Lord Jesus Christ. Born in Edgecombe County, North Carolina, Johnson grew up in abject poverty and worked as a sharecropper on a cotton farm. He encountered holiness at an early age in Halifax, NC. Johnson moved to Philadelphia in 1917, and there he was introduced to baptism in Jesus' name. After hearing the Apostolic message, Johnson was baptized at the Apostolic Faith Assembly organized by Henry Prentiss.

A few years later, in 1919, Johnson joined the Church of Our Lord Jesus Christ of the Apostolic Faith founded by Robert C. Lawson. Lawson ordained Johnson as an elder in 1920 and assigned him to the Philadelphia Church of Christ in North Philadelphia. Lawson elevated him to state overseer over Pennsylvania and North Carolina. By 1930, Johnson had built his church into the second-largest Pentecostal congregation in Philadelphia. However, within a short period, Johnson protested Lawson's liberal policy concerning women's attire and role in ministry.

In 1933, Johnson split with COOLJC, taking North Carolina and Pennsylvania churches. His organization stressed women's head coverings and forbade them to straighten their hair. He also insisted that women wear long dresses and men wear dark-colored suits and be clean-shaven. In addition, his organization prohibited the observance of holidays such as Christmas and Easter.

A staunch proponent of water baptism in Jesus' name, Johnson openly challenged his critics to debate him on his popular radio broadcast, "The Whole Truth," which aired to over ninety stations throughout the United States, Haiti, Bahamas, Great Britain, and Portugal. Johnson also established restaurants, grocery stores, and a farm in Cherry Hill, New Jersey, where members of his church worked. With his numerous initiatives, Johnson was voted one of the most widely listened to African American preachers in America in the July 1949 issue of Ebony magazine. While on an evangelistic tour in Jamaica, British West Indies, Johnson died at age sixty-three. At his death, COTLJC had over 100 churches and 50,000 members in the United States, Canada, and the Caribbean.

Further Reading:

Church of the Lord Jesus Christ. *Condensed Manual of the Doctrines, Rules and By-Laws of the Church of the Lord Jesus Christ of the Apostolic Faith.* Philadelphia, PA: Church of the Lord Jesus Christ, 1944.

McEady, Vivian. "History of the Founder: Biography of Bishop Sherrod C. Johnson, 1919–1950." The Church of the Lord Jesus Christ of the Apostolic Faith. Online: http://www.apostolic-ministries.net/late_bishop_johnson.htm.

Pearl Williams Jones 1931-1991

Musicologist, Educator, singer, writer, and musician was born in Washington, DC, to Smallwood E. Williams, the founder of Bible Way Church of Our Lord Jesus Christ, and Verna L. Williams. Pearl was baptized and filled with the Holy Spirit at eight. A member of the Church of Our Lord Jesus Christ she served as President of the Young Peoples' Union. She also served as the vice president of the Bible Way World Wide Youth Congress

in 1959. Pearl attended public schools in the District of Columbia, graduating from Charles Young Elementary, Brown Junior High School, and Dunbar High School. She earned a Bachelor's and Master of Music degrees at Howard University while studying with Hazel Harrison and Natalie Hinderas.

In 1972, she was awarded an honorary doctorate from Lycoming College in Pennsylvania. She made her debut as a singer and pianist in Town Hall, New York, in 1966. Jones traveled throughout the United States and Europe following her debut, appearing at the Kennedy Center in Washington, D.C., Carnegie Hall in New York City, London's Wigmore Hall, and Suphiensalle in Munich, Germany.

A scholar of gospel music, Jones taught at the University of the District of Columbia for eighteen years. She developed the first-degree program in the United States to study and perform gospel music. As a historian of gospel music, she made a significant contribution to the documentary film "Say Amen, Somebody," the story of the life of Mahalia Jackson. Dr. Jones also served as Director of Music at Bible Way Temple in Washington, DC. Her research in Black music was published in many scholarly journals.

Robert Clarence Lawson 1883-1961

Robert C. Lawson was one of the most influential Apostolic pioneers, a prolific hymn-writer, civil rights leader, and founder of the Church of Our Lord Jesus Christ. Lawson was born in New Iberia, Louisiana. His Aunt Peggy Frazier raised him after the death of his parents. In 1913, Lawson became terminally ill in Indianapolis with tuberculosis, which was untreatable. While in the hospital, a member of the Apostolic Faith Assembly invited him to her church. Lawson was miraculously healed of tuberculosis and filled with the Holy Spirit under the leadership of G. T. Haywood.

He joined Pentecostal Assemblies of the World in 1914. Haywood sent him to Columbus, Ohio, to pastor the Apostolic Faith Assembly, initially founded by Albert Roberts. By 1915, the Oneness Apostolic revival had spread in the Midwest. Lawson, who had an evangelistic zeal, carried the doctrine to Leavenworth, Kansas. The Pentecostal Church, founded by Mother Belle Davis, embraced Oneness Pentecostalism after hearing Lawson's message. Carrie Fields, a member of the small congregation, would marry Lawson in 1914 in Columbus, Ohio.

Lawson established several PAW churches under the title "Churches of Christ." In San Antonio, Texas, he founded Lincoln

Park Church of Christ. Dunlap Chenault became the pastor of Lincoln Park. He also introduced baptism in Jesus' name to members of Central Baptist Church in St. Louis, Missouri. From this group, Lawson organized the Temple Church of Christ. His evangelistic campaign led him south, where he met Thomas J. Cox, the founder of the Christian Faith Band, a holiness organization founded in 1897 in Danville, Kentucky. Cox adopted Oneness Pentecostalism after his encounter with Lawson.

One of the early black leaders of PAW, Lawson served as a field superintendent and on the General Board of Elders. In 1919, he resigned from PAW over the issue of divorce and remarriage. During the time, Lawson traveled to Harlem, New York City, founded Refuge Church of Christ, and continued to pastor his Ohio congregation, beginning with prayer meetings and street preaching services.

Lawson's ministry served as the launching ground for numerous preachers, ministers, and missionaries between 1920 and 1930. In 1931, he incorporated his organization and renamed the body Church of Our Lord Jesus Christ. Lawson stressed formal education for his ministers and preachers within the growing organization. He launched the Church of Christ Bible Institute in 1926 and a boarding school in Southern Pines, North Carolina that became known as the R. C. Lawson Institute in 1951.

During tough economic times for African Americans in Harlem, Lawson created a grocery store, nursery school, bookstore, and a chain of funeral homes called the "People's Funeral Home." In addition, he established an "all black" community known as Lawsonville in Shrub Oaks, New York. The community consisted of a grocery store, printing press, funeral home, and a farm.

Lawson became a nationally known preacher when he began his radio broadcast on WGBS. Because of his popularity, he was named one of the top preachers in America by Ebony magazine in 1949. His first wife, Carrie Lawson, known as the "Praying Mother of the Air," died in 1948. In 1952, Lawson married Evelyn Burke, a PAW evangelist and COOLJC missionary who founded COOLJC's Ministers and Wives Guild.

A civil rights leader, he worked with Senator Adam Clayton Powell, Jr., and he attended the first Civil Rights march in Washington, DC, on March 17, 1957, organized by A. Phillip Randolph and Reverend Dr. Martin Luther King. Lawson gained international attention in 1950 with his visit to Ethiopia. He served as the president of the Ethiopian World Federation. In 1954, Halie Selassie, the Emperor of Ethiopia, visited Lawson's home and awarded him the Star of Ethiopia.

Lawson was an early black theologian; his work, *The Anthropology of Jesus Christ Our Kinsman,* challenged racism in the Pentecostal movement and the broader society. In addition to his written work, Lawson penned several hymns, including "His Should Be Praised," "Let the Redeemed Say So," and "God is Great in My Soul." His songs became popular in black Apostolic congregations throughout the nation.

In 1957, Smallwood E. Williams, who pastored the second largest church in COOLJC, split with his "spiritual father." Williams formed the Bible Way Church of Our Lord Jesus Christ World Wide. One year after Williams and over seventy churches departed from the organization, Lawson held a summit meeting at Refuge Temple in New York. The convocation convened to unify the broken organization.

In a sermon titled "Add Thou to It," Lawson challenged his successors to improve upon his work, including 175 churches and 50,000 members in the United States, Trinidad, Jamaica, and Africa. Lawson died in July 1961; he contributed to Oneness theology, hymnody, and, most notably, to the overall spread and development of the movement. The organization he founded would birth over twenty black Apostolic bodies.

Further Reading:
Stewart, Alexander C., and Sherry Sherrod DuPree. *The Silent Spokesman: Bishop Robert Clarence Lawson.* Gainesville, FL: Displays for Schools, 1994.

Austin Augustus Layne, 1891-1967

One of the founding fathers of the Apostolic movement in St. Louis, Missouri, was born in Barbados, West Indies. Layne moved to New York City in 1913 at the age of twenty-two. He received his early education in Barbados but later studied theology at Columbia University in New York. He also attended Shelton College of New York (formerly known as the National Bible Institute) and the Moody Bible Institute in Chicago, Illinois.

While walking down Fifth Avenue, Layne overheard a young woman, Naomi Waller, the sister of Thomas Fats Waller, giving her testimony during a street revival. Touched by what he heard, he attended King's Chapel Assembly and was introduced to the Apostolic doctrine through the ministry of Susan Lightford. Soon after, Layne, who grew up an Episcopalian, received the baptism of the Holy Spirit and was baptized in the name of Jesus.

Layne began preaching on the street corners of New York. Sometime in 1918, Robert C. Lawson sent him to pastor Temple Church of Christ, the church he founded in St. Louis, Missouri. On his way to St. Louis, Layne and his wife, Selena, visited Joseph M. Turpin in Baltimore, Maryland. First, Apostolic Faith Church closed due to an influenza epidemic; therefore, services were held in

Turpin's home. Layne arrived in St. Louis and pastored a small storefront church with twelve members in November.

His congregation grew to become one of the largest Pentecostal churches in the city and moved into a 500 seated edifice in 1948. By 1950, several works were established in the region because of Layne's influence. As a result, he proposed forming a district council known as the Midwestern District Council in 1951. Layne served as president until his passing at seventy-six years of age.

Samuel Austin Layne, Sr. 1891-1967

The son of Pentecostal Assemblies of the World's early leader, Augustus Augustin Layne, was a native of St. Louis, Missouri. He attended Northwestern University and Kansas University, studying as a concert violinist. In 1967, he succeeded his father as pastor of Temple Church of Christ. He rose within the ranks of PAW, serving as General Treasurer and district elder. In 1980, he was appointed to the office of bishop and diocesan over the 36th Episcopal District of the Eastern Caribbean District Council. Layne was more than a church leader; he was also an influential community leader who worked as board commissioner of the St. Louis Housing Authority. For over thirty years, Layne pastored the historic Temple Church of Christ in St. Louis.

Clester Richard Lee 1896-1991

Born in Hart County, Kentucky, Lee moved to Marion, Indiana. He served in World War I. After returning, he relocated to Mansfield, Ohio, and launched a cleaning service. Lee converted to the Christian faith at Allen Temple AME in Marion. He embraced the Apostolic doctrine and was baptized in Jesus' name by Oscar H. Sanders in 1930. Five years later, he acknowledged his call to the ministry. Lee took over the leadership of the Apostolic Church of Christ and led the congregation for over forty-three years. He served in the position of District Elder, treasurer, Suffragan bishop, and chairman of the Ohio District Council. He was elevated to the bishopric in 1967 and presided over the Tri-State Council and 10th Episcopal District.

Willie Lee 1901-1969

The second presiding bishop of Pentecostal Churches of the Apostolic Faith was born in Starksville, Mississippi, but he migrated to Indianapolis, Indiana. After relocating to Detroit, Lee was appointed assistant pastor to Samuel N. Hancock at Greater Bethlehem Temple. Sometime later, he served as the pastor of Christ Temple in Muskegon Heights, Michigan, before returning to Indianapolis to pastor Christ Temple after the departure of Morris Golder in 1954.

In 1957, Lee left PAW and joined the newly formed PCAF and Hancock, Heardie Leaston, and David Collins, initially serving as the assistant presiding bishop. After the death of Hancock in 1963, he was elevated to the office of presiding bishop. One year after his appointment, Lee resigned from the position due to his controversial teaching concerning the divinity of Jesus. Following his resignation, he established the Emmanuel Pentecostal Church of Our Lord, Apostolic Faith in Indianapolis, and served as presiding prelate until he died in 1969.

George Grover Levant 1899-1974

The founder of Pentecostal Followers of Jesus Christ was born in Hendersonville, South Carolina. Levant moved to Baltimore, Maryland, and worked as a laborer at Bethlehem Steel. He joined First Apostolic Faith Church under the leadership of Bishop Joseph M. Turpin in 1925. Levant founded the First Apostolic Faith Gospel Tabernacle Church in 1931.

He left PAW and organized Pentecostal Followers of Jesus Christ in 1950. Levant presided over the organization for twenty-four years. After he died in 1974, Jobie Boone succeeded him as the presiding bishop. Winfred B. Hamlet serves as the current presiding prelate of the organization. PFJC has congregations in Maryland, Virginia, Georgia, Florida, North Carolina, Connecticut, London, England, and the Philippines.

Susan Gertrude Lightford 1878-1949

Prominent pastor, evangelist, and founder of King's Chapel Assembly in Harlem, New York, was born in Washington, DC. However, her family moved to New York and attended the Abyssinia Baptist Church, pastored by Reverend Adam Clayton Powell, Sr. She later attended a small Pentecostal church led by William Sturtevant, who visited the Azusa Street Revival in 1906 and founded the first Pentecostal church in New York. After she received the baptism of the Holy Spirit, Lightford began preaching on the streets of Harlem before launching King's Chapel Assembly in 1909.

Lightford first heard the Apostolic message in 1917 through the ministry of Henry Prentiss, an early Pentecostal evangelist. She did not initially embrace the doctrine but was later baptized by L. C. Hall in the Harlem River. After adopting Oneness Pentecostalism, she joined PAW and worked closely with G. T. Haywood. Lightford traveled with Haywood and his family on mission trips throughout the Caribbean and Israel. She was also an Eastern District Council member, serving on the Banking Committee.

King's Chapel membership reached over 200. Her flourishing congregation included Edward and Naomi Waller, the father and sister of jazz musician and composer Thomas (Fats) Waller, who also attended the church. Prominent ministers who received the baptism of the Holy Ghost under Lightford's ministry included Randolph A. Carr, founder of the Church of God in Jesus Christ (Apostolic), Peter J. F. Bridges, and Austin A. Layne Sr.

Further Reading:
Sims, Jane Ann. Telling our Story: A Brief History of Women in the Pentecostal Assemblies of the World. S.l.: J. Sims, 2003.

Lillian Mason 1890-1974

Lillian Mason was born in Munfordville, Kentucky, but migrated to Indianapolis, Indiana. In 1922, Mason founded a small church in her home in Indianapolis. First known as the Pentecostal Assembly of Christ Temple, the church was later renamed Christ Temple#2 after the "mother church" in Indianapolis. Mason affiliated with Pentecostal Assemblies of the World and became a leading member of the Apostolic Bible Student Association, a council governed by PAW ministers based in the Midwest. In 1957, she left PAW and joined Pentecostal Churches of the Apostolic Faith organized by Samuel N. Hancock.

Though she faced many obstacles and hardships, Mason successfully directed the construction of a two-story edifice where the church would worship for over thirty years. She pastored the church for forty-four years and retired in 1966. James O. Franklin succeeded her as pastor in 1967 and renamed the church Mt. Zion Apostolic Church. Bishop Lambert W. Gates, who took over as pastor in 1988, now serves as the presiding bishop of Pentecostal Churches of the Apostolic Faith.

Robert James McGoings 1917-2002

Robert J. McGoings was born in Baltimore, Maryland, and raised in Philadelphia and South Baltimore. He graduated from Douglas High School and studied at Morgan State College. McGoings found employment as a dining car porter at the B&O Railroad in 1937. He joined First Apostolic Faith Church there; he gained a reputation as a Bible Scholar gifted in memorizing the Scriptures.

McGoings amassed a vast library of artifacts from various Apostolic churches and organizations throughout his life. In 2002, the Society for Pentecostals Studies dedicated the 29th annual meeting papers to him for his commitment to preserving African American Apostolic history. In addition, McGoings donated some of his collection to the African American Holiness-Pentecostal Collection at Schomberg Center for Research in Black Culture in New York.

His son, who served as Principal Deputy Chief Immigration Judge of the United States, donated his father's collection, including publications, sermon notes, church programs, audio recordings, and other materials, to the Flower Pentecostal History Collection of the Assemblies of God.

Robert William McMurray 1926-1994

Born in Cincinnati, Ohio, the influential preacher, pastor, and bishop of Pentecostal Assemblies of the World was widely known for his popular recorded sermons such as "The Great Commission" and "Tell Rachel Not to Weep and the Church not to Mourn." McMurray was saved and baptized at the First Pentecostal Church in Cincinnati. He was called into the ministry at the age of twenty-three in 1949 and attended Moody Bible Institute and Aenon Bible College. As PAW's National Evangelist, McMurray traveled extensively throughout the United States. His tent revival meetings drew large crowds resulting in the baptism of hundreds.

In 1962, he became the pastor of Bethany Apostolic, renamed Bethany Community Church in Los Angeles, California. Under his leadership, the congregation grew from 100 people to over 5,000 members. McMurray was elevated to the bishopric in 1973 and served as Diocesan of the California District Council, founding over sixteen churches. He also led the Oklahoma State Council for four years.

The progressive leader helped over two thousand families during the 1992 riots and worked to bring peace among warring gangs in Compton, California. He also created the Greater

Bethany Economic Corporation, a 115-housing unit for low-income families. He was awarded a Doctorate of Humanities Degree from Aenon Bible College, a Doctor of Sacred Letters from the Fundamental Bible Seminary of Claremore, and a Doctor of Literature Degree from the City University in Los Angeles. McMurray's "spiritual son, Bishop Noel Jones, is City of Refuge's pastor (formerly known as Greater Bethany Community Church).

Marian B. Miller 1895-1974

Born in Washington, DC, Miller resided in Cincinnati, Ohio as a young person but returned to DC at thirty. Upon her return, she attended the Church of Jesus Christ founded by Lena Sears in 1929, where she was saved and baptized in Jesus' name in 1934. A few years later, Miller was ordained as a minister in PAW and served as assistant pastor and later interim pastor after Sears left the pastorate due to illness in 1950. Miller was installed as the full-time pastor in 1954. She left PAW in 1957, joined the newly formed Pentecostal Churches of the Apostolic Faith, and served as one of the Eastern and Southern States Council leaders. Miller led the Church of Jesus Christ for twenty years until she died in 1974.

Further Reading:
Noble, Earl M. *And They yet Speak: Historical Survey of African American Pentecostal-Holiness Churches in the Nation's Capital, Washington, D.C., 1900-2006*. Washington, D.C: Middle Atlantic Regional Press, 2007.

Mary E. Mills 1894-1962

Mary Mills founded one of the largest Pentecostal churches in Virginia. Born in Halifax County, Virginia, Mills initially grew up in the Baptist tradition and attended Traynham Grove Baptist Church in Lennig, Virginia. Then, she moved to Detroit, Michigan, where she entered the ministry. Next, Mills traveled to Columbus, Ohio, and served as an evangelist at the Emmanuel Tabernacle Baptist Church Apostolic Faith, founded by Martin R. Gregory.

In 1932, she relocated to South Boston, Virginia, and began holding worship services at the Independent Warehouse. One year later, she established Mayfield Apostolic Holiness Church. Her dynamic preaching and healing ministry drew both black and white people. With a membership of over 1,200, her church was one of the largest interracial Pentecostal churches in Virginia. Mayfield Apostolic Holiness Church was destroyed by fire in 1952 but was restored with the assistance of PAW's Virginia State Council. A civic leader, Mills was active in South Boston's local government and community.

Benjamin Thomas Moore 1927-1988

A native of Toledo, Ohio, the Pentecostal Assemblies of the World bishop founded the Northwest District Council and Christ Temple Academy. Like most young men during the 1940s, he served in the United States Army. After returning from World War II, Moore accepted his call into the ministry in 1946. Following his call, he attended and graduated from Butler University in Indianapolis, Indiana, with a Bachelor of Arts degree in Religion and Sociology.

He traveled as a National Evangelist for many years before accepting a position as a teacher at Aenon Bible College. Moore pastored Bethel Christian Church for twenty-five years. He organized the Pacific Northwest District Council and later served as the diocesan of the first Episcopal district of New York and Ontario, Canada. He was elevated to the office of bishop in 1961 and appointed pastor of Christ Temple, "The Mother Church" in Indianapolis. As pastor of the church once led by the Apostolic pioneer, G. T. Haywood. Moore pushed the city of Indianapolis to have the Fall Creek Parkway renamed the "Bishop Garfield T. Haywood Memorial Way.

Clarence E. Moore 1930-2020

Dora Belle Moore 1932-2014

Leader of the Virginia State Council of Pentecostal Assemblies of the World was born in Gary, West Virginia. At age eighteen, Moore began working as a coal miner for U.S. Steel, and he continued there for twenty-one years. In 1969, he retired from U. S. Steel and devoted himself full-time to the ministry and the pastorate. Moore married Dora Bell Moore in 1951 and began his ministry at Apostolic Temple in Gary in 1952.

He became the Greater Mt. Zion Pentecostal pastor in Bluefield, West Virginia, one year later. He led the congregation for sixty-seven years. Moore also served as Bishop of PAW's Virginia State Council for twenty-five, retiring in 2019. Before this, he served for six years as Chairman of the International Missions Department and as Assistant General Treasurer. Former presiding bishop Charles H. Ellis awarded Moore 2014 the "Presider's Award" for his years of service . His wife, Dora Bell, served as state Mother for the Virginia State Council and director of the West Virginia Council of Southern Mountains Community Action Program.

Joseph Moore -1966

Bishop Joseph Moore was one of the five founding fathers of the Bible Way Church of Our Lord Jesus Christ. He was converted at the Refuge Temple in Harlem, New York, under Robert C. Lawson. For over ten years, Moore served as assistant pastor at Refuge Church of Christ in Brooklyn, New York, while simultaneously working at the Brooklyn Navy Yard. In 1943, he left that congregation to start Bibleway Church of Our Lord Jesus Christ in Brooklyn.

In 1957, Moore split with COOLJC and joined Smallwood E. Williams, Winfield A. Showell, McKinley Williams, and John S. Beane to form the Bible Way Church of Our Lord Jesus Christ. After his consecration to the office of bishop, he served as the first Diocesan of New York, New Jersey, Connecticut, and Massachusetts. Moore earned his Doctor of Divinity in 1959. Huie L. Rogers succeeded him as pastor of Greater Bible Way Temple after his death in 1966.

James Thomas Morris 1892-1959

The founder of Highway Christian Church of Christ in Washington, DC, was born in Mount Carmel, South Carolina. Morris moved to Washington DC in 1922. One year after he arrived in DC, he attended and received the baptism of the Holy Spirit at a revival service conducted by Samuel Kelsey, who pastored the Temple Church of God in Christ. Morris joined Pentecostal Assemblies of the World in 1926. He founded Highway Church of Christ in 1927, beginning with a tent ministry and then moving into a storefront building before occupying a more substantial structure in 1937.

Within PAW, he served as vice-chairman of the DC, Maryland, and Delaware Council (formerly known as the Eastern District Council). In 1941, Morris left PAW and was consecrated as a bishop by Bishop Joseph M. Turpin. That same year, he launched the Highway Christian Churches of Christ and moved his headquarters from DC to New York. In 1959, his organization had forty-three churches throughout DC, New York, Virginia, Florida, North Carolina, and South Carolina at the time of his death.

Nathan Neal (E.N.) 1900-1964

The second presiding bishop of the Church of God, Apostolic, was born in Casville, North Carolina. Neal served as pastor of Saint Peters Apostolic Church of God and state overseer of Virginia. Thomas J. Cox first selected Neal to preside in his stead for an interim period. At Cox's death in 1943, he was succeeded by M. Gravely and Eli N. Neal as co-presiding bishops. Two years later, Gravely divorced his wife and remarried, and as a result, he was disfellowshipped from the church. As a result, Neal assumed the position of presiding bishop.

He served as presiding bishop until 1964. Neal's authoritarian leadership style led to a schism in the organization, with several leading pastors leaving to form a new body, the Apostle Church of Christ in God. Neal continued as bishop of the original organization until his death in 1964 in Forsythe, North Carolina.

Floyd Edward Nelson 1937-2019
Yvonne Nelson

Floyd E. Nelson served as the presiding bishop of the International Bible Way Church of Jesus Christ from 2014 to 2019. Born in Muskegon, Michigan, Nelson began his ministry at a very young age and was affiliated with the Pentecostal Assemblies of the World. While attending college, he supplemented his resources by working his way through school as a chef. Before he relocated to Washington, DC, he established churches in Texas, Missouri, Illinois, and California.

Shortly after arriving in DC, he established the Lively Stone Church of God, known as Kingdom Harvest Ministries. Nelson was consecrated to the Bishopric in 1976 in the Apostolic Assemblies of Christ and became affiliated with the Bible Way Church of Our Lord Jesus Christ in 1985. Within the Bible Way organization, he served on the Joint Board of Bishops and the Executive Board of Bishops. In 2006, Nelson was consecrated as an Apostle and First Vice-Presiding Bishop of International Bible Way. He was later appointed Bishop of Global Missions, serving churches worldwide.

In 2008, he and His wife, Dr. Yvonne Nelson, established a church in Nantucket, Massachusetts, located off the coast of Cape

Cod. He was elected to the office of Presiding Bishop of International Bible Way Church of Jesus Christ in 2014. His wife served as the president of the International Clergy Wives and Widow's Association during his administration. One of his major accomplishments was the consecration of the first woman, Bonnie Hunter to the office of bishop. Nelson led the organization from 2014 to 2019.

Earl Parchia Sr. 1927-2010

The founding pastor of Mt. Zion Assembly Healing Temple in Milwaukee, Wisconsin, was born in Stephens, Arkansas. Parchia was saved in 1945 under the ministry of John S. Holly and called to preach in 1947 in Chicago, Illinois. He traveled to Milwaukee and became the pastor of a small mission which came to be known as Mt. Zion Assembly Healing Temple after his honorable discharge from the Army.

Within PAW, Parchia rose through the ranks, serving as District Elder, Chairman of the Foreign Missionary Department, and Auxiliary Director of the International Women Workers' Auxiliary. He was elected to the office of bishop in 1968 and presided over 29th Episcopal District. In addition, Parchia worked on the Commission of Community Relations in Milwaukee for over ten years within the civic arena. He received degrees from Moody Bible Institute, Roosevelt University, United Armed Forces Institute, and an honorary doctorate from Aenon Bible College.

James Walter Parrott 1923-1997

The humanitarian, community activist, and Church of Our Lord Jesus Christ bishop was raised and educated in Pittsburgh, Pennsylvania. He joined the United States Army and served in World War II in the Pacific. Parrott found employment at the Veterans Administration and the US Air Force before entering the ministry. Shortly after, Robert C. Lawson sent him to Cliffwood, New Jersey, to work under the ministry of E. S. Harris, where he served as a Deacon and the Minister of Music.

In 1963, he established Lighthouse Temple Church in Newark, New Jersey. He rose in the ranks of COOLJC and first served as District Elder and was consecrated Bishop of the Metropolitan Diocese of New Jersey. Parrott's humanitarian work began in 1982 in Newark. He opened a soup kitchen that fed over five hundred people daily. His outreach ministry provided thousands of poor and homeless food, shelter, clothing, healthcare, job counseling, and spiritual support. His work among the poor and homeless did not go unnoticed. In 1996, the Governors of Rutgers University conferred upon him the Doctorate of Humane Letters. He was also recognized as one of the most influential people in New Jersey.

Joseph Paulceus 1893-

The Pentecostal Assemblies of the World bishop and missionary to Haiti was born in Damassin Sud, Haiti. He was saved in 1923 at the Church of God in Christ in Bridgeport, Connecticut. COGIC ordained Paulceus to the office of elder and commissioned him as a missionary to Haiti in 1928. One year after his arrival, he established the first COGIC congregation on the island. Paulceus left COGIC and joined PAW. He was consecrated as a bishop in 1950 and presided as the diocesan over Haiti for over forty years. During the time, he founded churches in Port-au-Prince, Leogane, and Petit Goave.

John W. Pernell 1914-1971

Founder of Refuge Temple Assemblies of Yahweh, a prominent leader in the Church of Our Lord Jesus Christ. Pernell was converted at nine years old at the Newark Gospel Tabernacle in Newark, New Jersey. Years later, Robert C. Lawson ordained him and sent him to Richmond, Virginia, in the early 1940s. His small congregation grew to over 400 members within a short period. Pernell was consecrated as a bishop and became the overseer of Virginia, North Carolina, West Virginia, Georgia, Florida, and Maryland. In 1963, he was elevated to the board of apostles, including William L. Bonner, Hubert J. Spencer, Maurice H. Hutner, and Henry Jones.

In 1969, Pernell split with COOLJC over what he considered a "new" revelation concerning the name of Jesus. Pernell believed the Old Testament name Yahweh should be referred to as God rather than the name of Jesus. His refusal to change this position brought about his exclusion from the COOLJC. He resigned from his pastorate to establish a new congregation in Richmond, Refuge Temple Assembly of Yahweh. Pernell presided over the organization briefly for two years.

Delphia Perry -1969

Mother Dellphia Perry established the International Women's Council in the Church of Our Lord Jesus Christ. She was a native of Fredericksburg, Virginia but resided in New York City, where she received the baptism of the Holy Spirit at Refuge Temple under Robert C. Lawson in 1933. Perry served as president of the Missionary Department and State Mother of Connecticut.

In 1951, she reportedly had a vision from God for a council of women workers. One year later, she organized the International Women's Council. The council's initial purpose was to raise funds, financially support foreign missions, and promote social concerns of women within the local congregations. In addition, IWC provided laywomen a voice for their problems and an arena to use their gifts and talents. Mother Perry served as the first president from 1952 to 1968.

Beverly D Pettiford (B. D.) 1863 - 1932
Emma Heil Pettiford 1869- 1954

Emma and B. D. Pettiford were founding leaders of the Oneness movement in the Southwest. The Pettifords heard about baptism in the name of Jesus while attending a tent revival meeting led by G. T. Haywood in Indianapolis, Indiana. The family left Indianapolis searching for a better climate for their daughter's illness. Traveling by covered wagon, the couple reached Albuquerque, New Mexico, five weeks after their departure from Indianapolis.

In 1922, she established God's House Church, the first Oneness Pentecostal church in Albuquerque. Her husband served as pastor, although he was not ordained. Shortly after, B. D. became an ordained minister. In 1927, he was appointed a District Elder in PAW, and a few years later, Emma received her ordination. When her husband died in 1932, she appointed Otho Pettiford, her son, the pastor in 1933. After her husband's death, Emma remarried and served in various capacities at the church until her death in 1954.

Otho Pettiford 1894-1973
Odell Greer Pettiford 1899-1963

A native of Marion, Indiana, Otho Pettiford served as a District Elder and Bishop in Pentecostal Assemblies of the World for thirty-two years. He was saved and baptized in the name of Jesus under the ministry of his parents, Emma and Beverly. D. Pettiford. Otho married Odell Greer in 1919. He was called to preach and affiliated with PAW in 1923. Pettiford succeeded his father as pastor of God's House Church in Albuquerque, New Mexico, in 1933. He later established PAW's Mountain State Council, including New Mexico and Arizona. Otho and his wife served the congregation for over forty years. For many years, Pettiford was also a building contractor and a member of the Bernalillo Sherriff's Department.

Lulu Lightey Phillips 1864-1939

Lulu Lightey Phillips was one of the founding leaders of the Glorious Church of God in Christ. Born one year after the emancipation of slaves in Centerville, Alabama, Phillips grew up a Baptist and was a member of the Good Hope Baptist Church. Elias Dempsey Smith, a former Methodist, organized Triumph the Church and Kingdom of God in Christ in 1902 in Baton Rouge, Louisiana. Influenced by *Ethiopianism* and Marcus Garvey's "Back to Africa" movement, Smith regarded himself as the "king of the Black race." In 1910, Phillips embraced Smith's Black Nationalist message and joined Triumph the Church. At forty-six, she accepted the call to ministry and began holding church services in Avondale, Alabama.

Phillips sensed the need to carry Smith's message to West Virginia, so in 1915, she moved to Huntington. By 1918, she planted churches in Mount Hope and Sun. In 1920, the founder of Triumph the Church died in Africa. Then, in 1921, leaders of the organization, including Phillips, Cleveland H. Stokes, and Sidney Coy Bass, met in Charleston to reorganize their group after the death of Smith. From this meeting, the Glorious Church of God in Christ was born.

Shortly after, Phillips heard about the Oneness movement in 1922. S invited Martin R. Gregory, the founder of Emmanuel Tabernacle Baptist Church, to speak in Huntington concerning baptism in Jesus' name and the Oneness of God. Afterward, Phillips and fifty members of her congregation were baptized. Glorious Church became a Oneness body following her baptism.

Phillips was elected General Mother in 1928, but the organization struggled after her death in 1939. In 1955, a schism occurred when several leaders left and formed the Original Glorious Church of God in Christ. Both organizations credit Mother Phillips's role in their founding.

Further Reading:
Payne, Leonard M. Jr. *My People Yesterday, Today and Forever: A History of the Glorious Church of God in Christ.* n.i.: Xlibris, 2008, 86.

William Thomas Phillips 1893-1973

Apostolic Overcoming Holy Church of God, founder, and the first presiding bishop, was born in the deep South in Birmingham, Alabama. His mother died when he was only eighteen months old. His father, a Methodist minister, raised Phillips. He was an active member of Methodism until he attended a revival tent meeting in 1912 led by Reverend Frank Williams, an early visitor to the Azusa Street Revival and close friend of William J. Seymour. Phillips received the baptism of the Holy Spirit and converted to Holiness. He joined Williams' church in Mobile, Alabama, and was called into the ministry in 1913. Phillips traveled throughout the South preaching as an evangelist. In 1916, he founded Adams Street Holiness Church in Mobile, AL. Shortly after he embraced the revelation of baptism in the name of Jesus, Phillips founded the Ethiopian Overcoming Holy Church.

Located in the Deep South at the height of racial segregation and the rise of Marcus Garvey, the Ethiopian Overcoming Holy Church endorsed an early "black theology" that promoted the empowerment of the black race. In 1941, to appear more inclusive to all nationalities, the organization officially changed its name to the Apostolic Overcoming Holy Church of God. Phillips lived in the epic center of the Civil Rights Movement. His involvement in the movement led to the bombing of his home in 1965. Throughout that period, Phillips traveled extensively, holding revivals and planting new congregations in cities across the southern United States. AOHC had grown to three hundred churches in the United States, India, West Africa, and the Caribbean by his death. He led AOHC for fifty-seven years.

Further reading
Phillips, W. T. *Excerpt from the Life of Rev. W.T. Phillips and the Fundamentals of the Apostolic Overcoming Holy Church of God, Inc.* s.l.: s.n., s.d.

Charles Edward Poole 1898-1984
Mattie Bell Robinson Poole 1903-1968

Charles and Mattie Poole were the founders of Living Witness of the Apostolic Faith, Inc. and Bethlehem Temple in Chicago, Illinois. One of the most remarkable healing evangelists in the Pentecostal movement, Mattie was born in Memphis, Tennessee, but moved to Chicago at thirteen after her mother's death. Mattie studied music at the Chicago Musical College and Chicago Conservatory of Music under the tutelage of Lawyer Glassman. Mattie's life dramatically changed when she began attending the Apostolic Faith Church under the leadership of A. R. Schooler. At the age of seventeen, she received the baptism of the Holy Spirit and was baptized in Jesus' name by G. T. Haywood. Shortly after her conversion, she received her call to the ministry.

Mattie married Charles E. Poole one year after her call. Born in Gillsville, Georgia, Charles was converted at twelve. He later moved to Chicago and joined the Olivet Baptist Church. In 1922, he embraced baptism in Jesus' name at Apostolic Faith Church and was called to preach sometime later. Charles served as assistant pastor until he and Mattie founded a storefront that grew to become Bethlehem Tabernacle, a congregation of several hundred, housing numerous ministries in a multi-auditorium facility.

Mattie's dynamic preaching drew numerous people, but her healing ministry was the main attraction at Bethlehem Tabernacle. Neck braces, walkers, wheelchairs, and crutches decorated the walls of her church as a testimony to her healing ministry. The Poole's ministry expanded in 1954 to include an international radio broadcast that reached over twenty-four markets throughout the United States. In addition, they traveled extensively in healing campaigns across the country, where thousands were baptized in Jesus' Name and healed. After many successful revivals, Mattie and Charles established Bethlehem Healing Temple and Bible Colleges in Atlanta, Brooklyn, and Boston.

In 1957, they left PAW and joined the Pentecostal Churches of the Apostolic Faith founded by Bishop Samuel N. Hancock. After the death of Hancock in 1963, they organized Living Witnesses of the Apostolic Faith, Inc. Mother Poole died in 1968, and Charles served as bishop over the organization until he died in 1984. By her death, Mattie had planted churches and Bible schools across the United States and in Ghana, Liberia, Nigeria, and Jamaica.

Henry Prentiss 1873-1934

An early Pentecostal leader and evangelist who was instrumental in spreading Oneness Pentecostalism was born in Stanton, Virginia, near the Shenandoah Valley. He, like many others, heard the news about the Azusa Street Revival in 1906 and traveled to Los Angeles to witness the experience for himself. As a result, Prentiss received the Pentecostal experience of spirit baptism and began preaching throughout California.

Along with other young men, he held nightly revival meetings in Whitter, California, a small town outside of Los Angeles. Later, Prentiss traveled to Pasadena, California, and Portland, Oregon. Prentiss held several successful revival campaigns in Portland with Florence Crawford, who worked with William J. Seymour.

In 1907, Glen A. Cook, a leader of the Azusa Street Mission and Pentecostal evangelist, sent Prentiss to Indianapolis to pastor a small group of individuals who had experienced the Baptism of the Holy Spirit. Because of his evangelistic zeal, the Apostolic Faith Assembly's membership quickly increased, and the church relocated to a larger building. In 1908, one of Oneness Pentecostals' most outstanding leaders, G. T. Haywood, visited the church. Prentiss convinced Haywood concerning the baptism of the Holy Spirit. After his conversion, Haywood joined the Apostolic Faith Assembly and worked alongside Prentiss.

In February 1909, Prentiss left the church for reasons unknown and turned over the leadership to Haywood. After leaving Indianapolis, Prentiss moved to Philadelphia, and there he founded the Apostolic Faith Assembly. He embraced Oneness sometime after 1913, and his church soon became the center of the Apostolic revival on the east coast.

Prentiss introduced the apostolic doctrine to leaders who impacted the Apostolic movement. Bishop Joseph M. Turpin, one of the original five bishops of PAW, visited Prentiss along with his wife, Mother Ruth Beatrice Turpin, in 1916. The couple was baptized in the name of Jesus afterward. Turpin organized the Apostolic Faith Church, the "first" Oneness Pentecostal church in Maryland one year later. Samuel J. Grimes, the second presiding bishop of PAW, and his wife Kathleen Grimes attended Apostolic Faith Assembly. Prentiss traveled to New York, where he introduced the doctrine to Susan G. Lightford, the founder of King's Chapel Assembly in Harlem, New York.

Prentiss' aggressive style of preaching resulted in several incidents and arrests. In mid-1906, he was nearly lynched for "disturbing the peace" at a tent meeting in Los Angeles when he pointed his finger at a white Church of God minister's daughter and declared her a sinner. In Atlantic City, New Jersey, he was arrested for "wild mannerism" while delivering a sermon in 1917. Little is known about the ministry of Prentiss during the 1920s. He resided in Chicago, Illinois, for a short period. In 1930, he attended the Church of Christ of the Apostolic Faith 11th Annual convention in New York and spoke briefly to the delegation. Prentiss died July 3, 1934, in Philadelphia, Pennsylvania.

Further Reading:
Golder, Morris E. *The Life and Works of Bishop Garfield Thomas Haywood (1880-1931)*. Indianapolis, IN: s.n., 1977.

Hyatt, Eddie L. *Fire on the Earth: Eyewitness Reports from the Azusa Street Revival*. Lake Mary: Creation House, 2006.

Hattie Edwards Pryor 1877-1954

Hattie E. Pryor wrote and composed "The Water Way" a few years after the initial rise of the Apostolic revival. The hymn became the definitive anthem of the Oneness Pentecostal movement. Pryor also arranged music for Robert C. Lawson's well-known hymns "Praise Thy Name," "Worthy is the Lamb," and "The Royal Nation." Born in Virginia, Pryor lived the remainder of her life in Cleveland, Ohio, where she died.

Viola Redd **1899-1971**

Pentecostal Assemblies of the World pastor and evangelist pioneered the Oneness Pentecostal movement in Tennessee. Viola Shelton Redd was born in the small town of Beaverdam, North Carolina, but her family moved to Tennessee sometime in 1917. In search of employment, the family moved to the mining town of Gary, West Virginia. Viola visited Emmanuel Tabernacle Baptist Church of the Apostolic Faith while in Gary in 1925.

Redd acknowledged her call and became a licensed minister under the leadership of Gregory in 1926. She relocated from West Virginia and moved to Johnson City, Tennessee, in 1928. There she established Grace Temple. Redd left Emmanuel Tabernacle Baptist Church and joined PAW. Her ministry spread throughout Tennessee within a short period. By her death in 1971, Redd was directly or indirectly responsible for the birth of six congregations, Jonesborough, Kingsport, Greenville, and Mountain City, Tennessee.

Jeremiah Reed 1930-2018
Willie Mae Reed 1934-2019

The founder of the Christ Apostolic Temple, Inc. Fellowship organization and the Apostolic Oneness Network television station was born in Nuyaka, Oklahoma. Reed served in the United States Army during the Korean War and received three bronze stars. In 1953, he met and married Willie Mae Wilson and moved to Omaha, Nebraska, in the early 1960s. The couple embraced Oneness Pentecostalism and later moved to Des Moines, Iowa. Reed became the pastor of Calvary Church of God in 1969. Within a short period, the membership grew from three to eighty. In 1975, the congregation moved into a new worship center that seated over five hundred.

He served as District Elder and Council Chairman in the 8th Episcopal District Tri-State Council of the PAW. In 1983, he was elevated to the office of bishop. Reed left PAW in 1997 and was appointed the presiding bishop of Jesus Christ Apostolic Churches Inc. He resigned from the organization and founded the Christ Apostolic Temple, Inc., Fellowship Organization in 2003. Headquartered in Des Moines, the organization launched congregations throughout the United States, Sierra Leone, Africa, the Philippines, and Pakistan.

Reed and his wife Willie Mae developed several community-based outreach programs, including the Eastside Community Substance Abuse Center, a youth offender program, a food pantry, and prison ministries. In the late 1970s, Reed started a television ministry. His successful broadcast led him to obtain a broadcasting license and establish the Apostolic Oneness Network (AON). He also authored several books, including *The Principles of the Apostolic Doctrine, The Foundation that Have Been Destroyed,* and *The Marriage Handbook.*

Hilda Reeder 1888-1971

One of the early women leaders of Pentecostal Assemblies of the World was born in Indianapolis, Indiana. Although she and her siblings were orphaned after the death of their parents, Reeder was reared in the Presbyterian tradition and attended the Witherspoon United Presbyterian, where she served as president of the Ladies Missionary Society.

In 1912, she received the baptism of the Holy Spirit at Fall Creek in Indianapolis. A few years after her Pentecostal experience, the Oneness revival reached Indianapolis. Reeder embraced the Apostolic doctrine and was baptized in Jesus' name at the Oak Hill Tabernacle in 1915. Following her baptism, she joined the Apostolic Faith Assembly under the ministry of G. T. Haywood.

Shortly after she joined his church, Haywood assigned Reeder to organize his foreign mission department. Haywood later appointed her the first National Secretary of PAW's Foreign Missions Department. Her exemplary work in foreign missions opened the door for leadership positions in PAW when women were not permitted to hold ecclesiastical offices. Reeder served as one of the first women members of PAW's Executive Board.

She held the office of Treasurer in the Foreign Missions department for twenty years until her retirement in 1951.

Further Reading:

Reeder, Hilda. *A Brief History of the Foreign Missionary Department of the Pentecostal Assemblies of the World.* Indianapolis: Foreign Missionary Dept, 1951.

James C. Richardson, Sr. 1910-1995

Born in Newberry County, South Carolina, the second presiding bishop of the Apostle Church of Christ in God left his hometown and traveled to Georgia, then to Florida, before moving to Winston Salem, North Carolina. Richardson embraced baptism in Jesus' name. He entered the ministry and served as assistant pastor at Saints Peters Church of God under the leadership of E. N. Neal. Neal, the General Overseer and presiding bishop of the Church of God Apostolic sent Richardson to Martinsville, Virginia, to pastor Mount Sinai in 1935.

The church was initially established as a prayer meeting and Bible study in the home of Mother Lucy Redd. Mount Sinai rapidly grew from a few members to a large congregation under the pastorate of Richardson. In 1941, Richardson, along with J. W. Ardrey, J. J. Jenkins, J. M. Williams, and W. R. Bryant split with COGA and organized the Apostles Church of Christ in God. He served on the Board of Elders and Bishops within the newly formed. Richardson was appointed presiding bishop of the organization in 1956 and he implemented several new initiatives, including the Apostolic Gazette's national publication, later renamed *The Apostolic Journal.* He also established the National

Scholar Program, an educational fund for African American high school students.

He funded education, and at the age of fifty-one, Richardson attended the Virginia University of Lynchburg to pursue a Bachelor's degree. He also enrolled in correspondent courses at Aenon Bible College in Columbus, Ohio. In addition, Richardson served as the presiding prelate of Apostles Church of Christ in God for thirty-nine years.

Further Reading:
Richardson, James C. *God's Chosen Prelate: The Life and Ministry of Bishop James C. Richardson, Sr.* Capital Heights, MD: Seymour Press, 2019.

Jasper Roby 1912-2006

The second presiding bishop of Apostolic Overcoming Holy Church was born in Brookfield, Mississippi, and resided in Demopolis, Alabama, for a short time. Roby became an ordained minister in 1942 and established the Greater Seventeenth Street Apostolic Overcoming Holy Church of God in Birmingham, Alabama. He was consecrated to the office of bishop in 1956. That same year, he received the B.Th. Degree from American Divinity School.

In 1963, a church bombing at the Sixteenth Baptist Church in Birmingham, Alabama, killed four young African American girls. Roby's church, located one block away on Seventeenth Street, was damaged during the blast. Roby became involved in the Civil Rights Movement and a lifelong member of the NAACP after the bombing.

Roby succeeded William T. Phillips, the founder of AOHC, as the presiding bishop after his death in 1973. He moved the church headquarters from Mobile to Birmingham, Alabama, and founded the AOHC Theological Seminary and Academic Studies. His sermons aired on several Birmingham radio stations for more than forty years, and he hosted the television program "The Bishop's Gospel hour" for more than eight years.

In 2000, when Roby became ill and unable to serve as presider bishop, George W. Ayers was elected by the National Executive Board. After a two-year legal battle when a fraction of leaders disagreed with his appointment, the Alabama Supreme Court named Ayers the rightful leader. Unfortunately, Roby died at ninety-five, four years after Ayers' appointment.

Sylvia Rose 1907-1986

Mother Sylvia Rose succeeded Geneva Shelton as President of the Missionary Department of Bible Way Church of Our Lord Jesus Christ in 1961. Born in Columbia, South Carolina, her family relocated to Pittsburgh, Pennsylvania, during the Depression in the 1930s. In 1956, she and her husband, William Rose, moved to New York, where they attended Refuge Church of Christ, led by Robert C. Lawson.

Years later, she moved to Peekskill, New York, and joined a small group of saints who held worship services in their home. This church would become known as the Refuge Church of Christ under the leadership of Charles Faulkner, who Lawson sent to pastor the church. In 1957, Faulkner left COOLJC and joined the Bible Way Church of Our Lord Jesus Christ.

Rose was appointed President of the Missionary Department in 1961 after Shelton became ill. That same year following her appointment, she was miraculously healed of cancer. Hundreds of people received the baptism of the Holy Ghost under her ministry. At the First Apostolic Faith Church in Baltimore, Maryland, over forty-two people were filled with the Spirit. She traveled to Brooklyn, New York, following her meeting in Baltimore, where over eighty-five received the Holy Ghost's baptism at Bible Way Church, pastored by Bishop Joseph Moore. In recognition of her work, in 1971, Mayor Michael J. DiBart, of Peekskill, New York, designated October 15 "Mother Sylvia Rose Day."

Further Reading
Rose, Sylvia. *The life and legacy of Mother Sylvia Rose*, n.p:, n.d.

Nina Ryan Russell 1888-1952

Nina Ryan Russell was a Jamaican lay evangelist who preached throughout the island, where she was instrumental in establishing the United Pentecostal Church. Mother Russell was born in Brown's Town, St. Anne, Jamaica. She was converted to the Pentecostal faith in 1914. After her Pentecostal experience of the Holy Spirit, Russell returned to her home parish and started a revival that spread to several neighboring towns in 1919.

She moved to Kingston in 1934, where she began conducting similar types of services at Goodwin Park in East Kingston as she had done in Brown's Town. In the 1930s, the Apostolic message had started to spread in Kingston. Russell requested early Oneness pioneer Andrew David Urshan visit Jamacia to baptize recent converts in the name of Jesus. Unable to come, Urshan sent Pentecostal Assembly of Jesus Christ preacher William T. Witherspoon from Columbus, Ohio, to Jamaica in 1934. That year, Russell and sixty-two people were baptized.

In 1940, her group became the first established work in Jamaica out of the official merger, which formed the United Pentecostal Church in 1945. This location became the nucleus from which Mother Russell launched outreach activities in the eastern section of the island, namely, St. Thomas, St. Catherine, and St. Mary. In 1952, she returned to Canada. However, one month later, she passed away. In 1986, Russel's family published her book about the history of the Oneness movement in Jamaica, which was primarily focused on the efforts of the UPC.

Further Reading:
Russell, J. C. "A Brief History of the United Pentecostal Church in Jamaica" *The Evening Light.* August 1986.

Wallace, Mary H. Profiles of Pentecostal Missionaries. Hazelwood: Word Aflame press, 1986.

Oscar Haywood Sanders 1892-1972
Hattie Belle Sanders

Pentecostal Assemblies of the World influential bishop and founder of Christ Temple Apostolic Church was born in Lanoke, Arkansas. His family later moved to Pine Bluff, Arkansas, in 1905. Sanders was a deeply religious teenager who found comfort in reading and studying the Bible.

Living in the South, he witnessed firsthand the brutality of racial injustice when two of his close friends were lynched. Sanders migrated from the segregated South to the Midwest in Indianapolis, Indiana, in 1913. While in Indianapolis, he attended Shiloh Baptist Church. He was introduced to the Apostolic message in 1918 and baptized in Jesus' name under the pastorate of G. T. Haywood.

He accepted the call to the ministry in 1918 and began preaching on the streets of Indianapolis. Sanders felt the need to take the Apostolic doctrine to Muncie, Indiana. He traveled to Muncie but only stayed in the city for ten days. A few years later, he was sent to pastor an "all-white" assembly in Frankfort, Indiana. The congregants rebelled against his ministry, and he returned to Indianapolis. He moved back to Muncie and organized

Christ Temple Apostolic Church in 1922. The congregation grew to become one of the largest integrated churches in Muncie.

Sanders moved into the leadership ranks of PAW after the failed merger with Pentecostal Assemblies of Jesus Christ. He became an influential member of the Apostolic Bible Student Association. Sanders was appointed to the office of bishop in 1948 and served as the overseer of the State of Indiana. He was best known for his sermons on holiness; thus, he became widely known as "Sin-killing Sanders." He miraculously escaped an attempt on his life while preaching at his church in 1972. The bullet fired pierced his hand and followed through his suitcoat sleeve out and the back of his chair. Sanders died a few months later at the age of eighty.

Further Reading:
Fairley, David L. *Moved by Such a Man.* Muncie, IN: n.p., 1980.

Monroe Randolph Saunders, Sr. 1919-2008
Alberta Brockington Saunders 1928-

The pastor of the First United Church of Jesus Christ Apostolic and the founder of the United Church of Jesus Christ (Apostolic), Saunders was born in Florence, South Carolina. He was a high school valedictorian and earned a Virginia State College for Negroes scholarship, now Virginia State University, in Petersburg, Virginia. However, after the death of his eldest brother, he left college and moved to Baltimore, Maryland, to help his sister-in-law raise their four children.

Raised in the Methodist Church, Saunders encountered Pentecostalism for the first time while visiting the Church of God in Christ#6. He received the baptism of the Holy Spirit and soon after entered the ministry. Under the mentorship of pastor Randolph A. Carr, Saunders edited and published COGIC#6 first newspaper, organized street services, and taught Sunday school and Bible class.

Saunders was drafted into the United States Army during World War II in 1942. After the war, he attended Howard University, earning a bachelor's degree in sociology and later a Master of Divinity degree. He also received a Doctor of Ministry degree from Howard. Saunders married Alberta Brockington in 1947. From this union were born six children.

He was ordained as a bishop in the Church of God in Christ Jesus Apostolic under Carr in 1957. However, Saunders split with his "spiritual mentor" and established the United Church of Jesus Christ (Apostolic) in 1965. As a community leader, Saunders worked with the late mayor of Baltimore City, William Donald Schaffer, to help revitalize poor urban neighborhoods. He served twelve years as a commissioner of the Baltimore City School system. An advocate for senior citizens' Saunders served on the Maryland State Commission on Aging and Retirement Education. In 2004 Saunders was consecrated chief apostle of the organization. In that year, his son, Monroe, took over as pastor of Transformation Church of Jesus Christ and presiding bishop.

Further Reading:
Saunders, Monroe R. *Sermons and Hymns from My Heart*. Enumclaw, WA: Pleasant Word, 2004.

Willard E. Saunders 1925-1994
Mary J. Saunders 1927-2013

A native of Sutherlin, Virginia, the prominent leader of the DC, Delaware, and Maryland District Council of the Pentecostal Assemblies of the World relocated to Baltimore, Maryland, in 1945. His family opened a barbershop, where he worked as a barber until he retired in 1963. Saunders was ordained at the age of eighteen at First Apostolic Faith Church under the leadership of Winfield A. Showell.

In 1954, Saunders founded Christ Temple Apostolic Church and established a bus service that developed into the S&P Bus Rental Company. He was appointed a bishop of PAW in 1981 and served as a member of the Executive Board of Bishops. One year later, he became the Diocesan leader over the DC, Delaware, and Maryland District Council. Saunders served as council leader from 1982 to 1986.

Further Reading:
D. C., Delaware, and Maryland District Council, 50TH Jubilee Year 1937-1987. n.p.: Pentecostals Assemblies of the World, n.d.

Alexander Robinson Schooler 1882-1950

One of the original five bishops of Pentecostal Assemblies of the World and the founder of the Apostolic Faith Church in Chicago, Illinois, was born in Lancaster, Kentucky. Schooler relocated to Indianapolis, Indiana, where he lived for a short period. Then, he left Indianapolis and moved to Cleveland, Ohio. There he organized the Pentecostal Church of Christ in 1915, that same year, he moved to Chicago and founded Apostolic Faith Church. Shortly after, he joined PAW and quickly moved into the organization's leadership ranks.

In 1918, Schooler, G. T. Haywood, F. I. Douglas and R. C. Lawson were the only four blacks to be elected to the office of Field Superintendent. Schooler also served as Vice General Chairman and Executive Vice-Chair. He was one of the founding fathers of the Ohio District Council and worked closely with Joseph M. Turpin to establish the Eastern District Council. After PAW was reorganized in 1925, he was elected one of the first original bishops of the organization and appointed to the Executive Board of bishops in 1927.

For a reason unknown, in 1931, he resigned as pastor of Apostolic Faith Church. John S. Holly replaced him as the pastor. Schooler left PAW and joined the Church of God in Jesus Christ

(Apostolic), founded by Randolph A. Carr in 1946. In addition to his leadership in PAW, Schooler wrote several Apostolic hymns. Some of his most noted compositions included "The Name," "God Died for Me," and "The Author and the Finisher."

David Schultz 1889-1973

Born in Mayfield, Kentucky, David Schultz moved to East St. Louis, Missouri, and later relocated to Wichita, Kansas, sometime in the 1920s. He and his wife, Grace, embraced baptism in Jesus' name in 1921. However, Schultz faced persecution in Casper, Wyoming, because of his Oneness stance. He later organized churches in Joplin, and Kansas City, Missouri, after his church was destroyed by fire in Wyoming. G. T. Haywood appointed him pastor of Bethel Temple Church in Louisville, Kentucky, in 1925 after the departure of Floyd. I. Douglas.

His popular radio broadcast on WLOU attracted many new converts, and Bethel Temple's membership multiplied. Schultz emerged as a prominent leader in PAW after the death of Haywood in 1931. He played a pivotal role in working with Samuel J. Grimes during the period of reorganization after several leaders left to join the Pentecostal Assemblies of Jesus Christ. In 1935, Schultz was elected to the office of bishop and served as the chairman of the Kentucky State Council.

Phillip Lee Scott 1907-1987

Born in Greenwood, Mississippi, Scott was converted at nine at Morning Star Baptist Church in Mound Bayou, Mississippi, in 1916. He traveled to St. Louis and embraced baptism in Jesus' name in 1921. Years later, Scott formed the Lively Stone Prayer Band, and from this group, Lively Stone Church of God was born in 1934. The church membership outgrew its building within a few years and moved into a larger edifice.

Scott expanded his ministry during the 1940s. He established Lively Stone Church in Nortonville, Kentucky, and served as the pastor of both locations in St. Louis and Nortonville for forty-six years. Sister congregations were also developed by Scott in California, Illinois, Oregon, and Mississippi. Within PAW, Scott served in various capacities, including District Elder, instructor of the Ministerial Board, Chairman of the convention committee, and Auxiliary Director of National Ministers' Wives Auxiliary. He was elevated to the bishopric in 1968 and served as diocesan of the Mid-Western District Council.

Lena Sears 1891-1974

The founder of the Church of Jesus Christ in Washington, DC., was born in 1891 in North Carolina. Sears's family moved to DC, but she later relocated to New York. Sears attended the Refuge Church of Christ in New York City. She received the call to ministry and soon left Refuge because Robert C. Lawson did not ordain women preachers. Sears moved back to Washington, DC, and established the Church of Jesus Christ. She joined PAW and was ordained in 1930. During the Great Depression, her church received funding from the Work Progress Administration (WPA) to musically train congregants. Thus, her church became one of the first Apostolic congregations to incorporate a full orchestra.

The church purchased a Jewish Synagogue in 1945, but Sears became seriously ill in 1950. When she could no longer carry out her pastoral duties, assistant pastor Marion Miller served as interim pastor until she was appointed pastor in 1954. Although Mother Sears died in 1974, her ministry produced numerous missionaries, evangelists, and pastors, in the greater metropolitan area of Washington, DC.

Geneva Shelton 1892-1961

The first president of Bible Way Church of Our Lord Jesus Missionary Department was born in Spartanburg, South Carolina, around 1892. Shelton moved to Washington, DC, with her husband Thomas Shelton and family after the 1920s. She joined Bible Way Church in Washington, DC, in 1937 and served as president of the Social and Senior missionaries. Bishop Smallwood E. Williams appointed her General President of the missionary department shortly after establishing the organization in 1957. Shelton added several auxiliaries to the Missionary Department, including the Field, Senior, Social, and Junior missionaries. Under her leadership, the department funded foreign missions in Liberia, West Africa, Jamaica, West Indies, and the Bahamas. Shelton resigned from the office in 1961 due to illness.

Samuel McDowell Shelton (S.M.) 1929- 1991

Samuel McDowell Shelton served as the second presiding Bishop and General Overseer of the Church of the Lord Jesus Christ of the Apostolic Faith. The Philadelphia native was raised by his maternal grandparents. He received his Bachelor of Arts in Sociology from Rutgers University and did graduate work at the University of Lisbon, Portugal. Shelton was awarded an honorary Doctor of Divinity by Bethune-Cookman College in Daytona Beach, Florida. He was fluent in German, Italian, French, Spanish, and Portuguese.

Shelton joined COTLJC and served as president of the National Young People's Department. Later, he was appointed General Secretary before the death of Bishop Sherrod C. Johnson in 1961. His ordination came a year after Johnson's death and a lengthy court battle prompted from within the organization. Shelton was elevated to the office of presiding bishop of the COTLJC at age 33.

Shelton brought prominence to the organization by expanding the group's radio broadcast, "The Whole Truth," to several languages and broadcasting it in the United States, Canada, Europe, Asia, and Africa over 62 radio stations in the Caribbean, Europe, Africa, and India. In addition, Shelton traveled globally, meeting with world leaders such as King Hussein of Jordan, Emperor Haile Selassie of Ethiopia; Pope Paul VI at the Vatican in Rome; and Prime Minister Indira Gandhi of India.

A strong proponent of education and black self-help, he founded the Apostolic Institute in 1967 and the Apostolic Summer Youth Work program. In 1971, he built Apostolic Village, a 32-unit independent living apartment complex for seniors, part of Apostolic square. In addition, new churches were built under Shelton's leadership in Newark, New Jersey, and Ellendale, Delaware. During the 1980s, Shelton's health began to fail, and his travel schedule and personal appearances gradually declined. Shelton died in Philadelphia at age sixty-two in 1991, after a long fight with diabetes.

Further Reading:
Williams, Shirley and Samuel McDowell Shelton. *Blessedness, the Greatest Miracle in My Life!: His Holy Apostolic Blessedness: A Man After God's Own Heart!* S.l: S. Wms Enterprises LLC, 2014.

Winfield Amos Showell 1907-1988
Genevieve Francis Showell 1912-1987

Winfield A. Showell, one of the founding fathers of Bible Way Church of Our Lord Jesus Christ World Wide, was born in Frankford, Pennsylvania. He spent his early childhood in Denton, Maryland, on the Eastern Shore but moved to Baltimore, Maryland, in the 1920s. Before entering the ministry, Winfield attended Morgan College and majored in Political Science with the ambition of becoming a lawyer. In 1936, he met and married Genevieve Francis Young. Born in Calvert County in 1912, Genevieve moved to Baltimore in 1923 and was the first person to be baptized at the Apostolic Faith Church on Eden and Monument in 1925.

Showell's ministry began under the tutelage of his uncle and the founder of the First Apostolic Faith Church, Bishop Joseph M. Turpin, for whom he served as a chauffeur. A few years after he married, Showell was ordained by James T. Morris, the founder of Highway Christian Church of Christ, in 1938. Samuel J. Grimes, presiding bishop of Pentecostal Assemblies of the World, ordained him again at the National Convention in 1940. He was appointed a District Elder in 1950.

Upon the death of Turpin in 1943, Showell assumed the pastorate of the First Apostolic Faith Church in 1944. During his tenure, he started a radio ministry in 1945, over which he was heard for more than forty years. He reorganized the Turpin School of the Bible in 1947 and established the Sons of Solomon Boys Club. For many years, Showell served as a Board member of the Baltimore City Fire Department, the National Association for the Advancement of Colored People (NAACP), and the Baltimore City Human Relations Commission.

In 1957, he attended the National Pentecostal Ministerial Conference held in Washington, DC. The Bible Way Church of Our Lord Jesus Christ, World Wide, was born from this conference. Showell, Smallwood E. Williams, Joseph Moore, John S. Beane, and McKinley Williams were consecrated as the founding bishops of the organization by PAW leader John S. Holly. Showell had the unique distinction from all the other founders of Bible Way. He was not a spiritual son of Robert C. Lawson; neither was he a former member of the COOLJC organization.

Showell served thirty years as vice presiding bishop and as Diocesan of the New Jersey Diocese, the Central Maryland and Delaware Diocese, the Ohio Diocese, and the Jamaica and West Indies Diocese. In 1960, he organized and served as president of the Apostolic Ministerial Alliance. He possessed a humble, fatherly spirit as a conciliator and excellent parliamentarian. Under his leadership, First Apostolic Faith Church membership grew to over a thousand.

Alfred Singleton 1928-2017

The fifth presiding bishop of Pentecostal Churches of the Apostolic Faith was born in Montgomery, Alabama. He moved to Detroit, Michigan, and was baptized in Jesus' name at Greater Bethlehem Temple, pastored by Samuel N. Hancock in 1949. During the Korean War, he served in the United States Army, receiving technical training as a dispensary and a medical technician. Singleton moved to Los Angeles, California, in 1958. One year after his arrival, he organized Greater Bethlehem Temple in Monrovia, California. He held the office of District Elder and was appointed a bishop in 1964. Singleton relocated to Lansing, Michigan, and became the pastor of Bethlehem Temple in 1972. Within PCAF, he served as the Diocesan of the State of Michigan and the Board of Bishops.

Singleton studied at La Salle University in Chicago, Illinois, and was later awarded an honorary doctorate in Theology. He also served as the Chief Executive Coordinator of the Midwest Apostolic Bible College. In 2000, Singleton succeeded D. Rayford Bell as presiding bishop of PCAF 2000 to 2007. Following his tenure as the presider of PCAF, Singleton established the Samuel N. Hancock Archival Museum at the Bread House International Ministries in Lansing, Michigan.

Francis Leonard Smith 1915-1995

The sixth presiding bishop of the Pentecostal Assemblies of the World was born in Ironspot, Ohio, and raised by his grandparents, who were Methodist ministers. In 1933, Smith attended a convention at the church pastored by his uncle, Karl F. Smith, where he received the Holy Spirit baptism. After a short stint as pastor in Springfield, Ohio, Smith became an instructor at PAW's Aenon Bible College in 1946.

From 1951 to 1992, when he retired with the title of pastor emeritus, he pastored the First Apostolic Church in Akron, Ohio. Smith was elevated to the Bishopric of the PAW in 1972 and appointed to the Southern Tri-State Council of Mississippi, Alabama, and West Tennessee. That year, he began a two-year term as assistant presiding bishop of the organization under Ross Paddock. In 1974, Smith became a presiding bishop, serving two three-year terms before leaving that office in 1980. He was appointed to the Third Episcopal Diocese in his home state of Ohio and served until the end of his life.

Helen Smith 1929-1999

Helen Smith was the founder, and the first presider of Cainhoy Miracle Revival Corporation was born in Beaufort, South Carolina. A few years after her conversion in 1944, she contracted tuberculosis. From 1947 through 1949, she was confined to the Pine Haven Sanatorium in Charleston, South Carolina. Helen was healed after thirteen operations in six years. In 1957 she became a member of the Church of Our Lord Jesus Christ.

Smith acknowledged her call to preach in 1968. That year she began with a small group in the home of Mother Moriah Howard of Cainhoy, South Carolina. The revival quickly spread, and they outgrew the house. The group relocated to a small shack in the same town. Smith was asked to stop her revivals because COOLJC did not acknowledge God calling women to preach. When she refused, Smith and eleven others were excommunicated from the organization. In 1969, she was ordained as the Apostle of the Cainhoy Miracle Revival Center. By her death, Smith established fifteen churches in the United States of America and two churches in Trinidad, West Indies.

Karl Franklin Smith 1892-1972
Josephine Anna Smith 1895-1976

The founder of Aenon Bible College and former pastor of the historic Church of Christ of the Apostolic Faith in Columbus, Ohio, was born in Zanesville, Ohio. Henry and Mary Smith's parents were ordained African Methodist Episcopal ministers. Like his parents, Smith joined the AME church. He received his call to the ministry and enrolled at Payne Theological Seminary of Wilberforce University in Wilberforce, Ohio. Shortly after, Smith became the pastor of a small congregation known as the "Columbus Mission" in Columbus.

He encountered some members from the Apostolic Faith Assembly in Columbus, who introduced him to baptism in Jesus' name and speaking in tongues. Karl first rejected the Apostolic teaching, but in 1915, he was baptized in Jesus' name. Smith left Zanesville and moved to Columbus. There he began attending the Apostolic Faith Assembly led by Robert C. Lawson. In 1915, he was ordained as an elder in PAW, and he served as assistant pastor to Lawson.

Lawson resigned from PAW over the issue of divorce and remarriage in 1919. That year, he moved to Harlem, New York, and he left the pastorate of the newly named Church of Christ of the Apostolic Faith in the hands of Smith. In 1919, Lawson organized Churches of Christ of the Apostolic Faith, and he appointed Smith the first general secretary of the organization in 1920. He split with Lawson and rejoined PAW, and he was elected general secretary in 1925.

After the death of PAW's first presiding, G. T. Haywood, Smith left the organization along with several prominent black leaders but later returned to PAW after racial tensions arose in Pentecostal Assemblies of Jesus Christ. Smith and LaBaugh H. Stansbury realized the need for PAW to establish an Apostolic Bible college. In 1940, the organization approved the proposal for the Aenon Bible College. The first class began in 1941, with an enrollment of 12 students. Smith, Samuel J. Grimes, Fred Clark, and Robin F. Tobin served on the first Board of Directors. Smith was appointed to the office of bishop in 1940. He briefly served as the bishop of the Northwestern District Council during the 1950s. Smith served as pastor of the Church of Christ of the Apostolic Faith for fifty years.

Further Reading:
Smith, Aaron J. *A Devout Man: Biography of Karl F. Smith, 1892-1972.* Atlanta, GA: JacLyn Enterprises, 1998.

Willie Mae Ford Smith 1902-1973

Gospel singer and evangelist was born in Rolling Fork, Mississippi. She was the seventh of fourteen children born to devout Baptist parents, Clarence and Mary Ford. Her family relocated to Memphis, Tennessee, and later settled in St. Louis, Missouri, in 1917. Around this time, her father formed the Ford Sisters Quartet, a gospel group that included Willie Mae and her three sisters, Mary, Emma, and Geneva.

The sisters traveled and performed throughout the Midwest during the 1920s. Smith later toured as a solo artist. In 1938, she left the Baptist church and became an ordained minister in the African Methodist Episcopal Zion Church. She later joined the Church of God Apostolic. As a minister and evangelist, Smith popularized what became known as "songs and sermonettes."

While on tour sometime in the 1930s, she met Thomas A. Dorsey, who many consider the "father" of modern-day gospel music. Smith worked with Dorsey to form the National Convention of Gospel Choirs and Choruses. From 1936 until the late 1980s, she served as director of the convention's Soloist Bureau, evaluating and coaching gospel singers such as Roberta Martin, Mahalia Jackson, and the O'Neal Twins.

She recorded her first recorded album in 1950. In 1972, Smith received national recognition after an appearance at the Newport Jazz Festival. She appeared in the 1981 gospel documentary film "Say Amen, Somebody" and received a National Heritage Award from the National Endowment for the Arts in 1988. Smith joined Lively Stone Apostolic Church in St. Louis under PAW bishop Phillip L. Scott. She continued to preach and perform at Lively Stone until the early 1990s.

Further Reading:
Dargan, William Thomas, and Kathy White Bullock. "Willie Mae Ford Smith of St. Louis: A Shaping Influence upon Black Gospel Singing Style." *Black Music Research Journal* 9.2 (1989) 249–70.

Frank S. Solomon 1922-2005

A native of North Carolina, Solomon later resided in Richmond, Virginia. He was introduced to the Apostolic doctrine at Refuge Church of Our Lord Jesus Christ under the ministry of John W. Pernell. His first pastoral position was at Refuge Church in Littlejohn, North Carolina. While pastoring, Solomon earned a Bachelor of theology and Doctor of Divinity degree from the University Bible College in Alma, Tennessee.

In 1952 he relocated to Atlanta, Georgia, and served as pastor of Refuge Temple for fifty-three years. Solomon was a prominent community leader. His partnership with the Atlanta Food Bank helped assist hundreds of families in north Atlanta. He was appointed to the office of bishop in 1962 and elected Chairman of the Board of Bishops in 1970. In addition, Solomon served on the Board of Apostles and as Supervisor of the Department of Education. He held the office of presiding bishop of COOLJC from 1992 to 1993.

Hubert Joseph Spencer 1902-1973
Helen Lee Spencer

The second presiding bishop of the Church of Our Lord Jesus Christ was born in Marytown, West Virginia. Spencer was raised in the Baptist Church and converted to the Christian faith as a boy of nine years at Rockville Baptist Church in Gary, West Virginia. By age seventeen, he had transitioned into the Pentecostal movement and had a Pentecostal experience and a call to ministry. His family later moved to Columbus, Ohio, where Spencer was introduced to the apostolic doctrine and baptized in the name of Jesus. He began his ministry in COOLJC as a traveling evangelist with Robert C. Lawson.

In 1925, Lawson formed the Rehoboth Temple Church of Christ. He turned the church over to Spencer in 1927. Spencer led Rehoboth for forty-six years. In 1961, after the death of Lawson, Spencer, William L. Bonner, and Maurice H. Hutner formed the Board of Apostles. The board elected him as the successor to Lawson. Although Spencer served from 1961 to 1973, illness limited his tenure as presiding bishop.

Cleveland H. Stokes 1887-1966

The co-founder and first general secretary of the Glorious Church of God in Christ was born in Connellton, West Virginia. He moved to Mount Hope, West Virginia, and encountered the holiness Triumph the Church and Kingdom of God in Christ under the ministry of Mother Lulu Phillips, who started several churches in Mount Hope. In 1921, Stokes relocated to the small mining town of Everville, West Virginia. While working as a coal miner, he organized a mission in his two-room home. Stokes and several former members of Triumph Church and the Kingdom of God in Christ founded the Glorious Church of God in Christ.

It was Stokes who coined the name of the organization. He was appointed the first general secretary of GCOGIC and ordained an elder in 1921. In 1922, he embraced Oneness Pentecostalism and was baptized in the name of Jesus. Within the new body, Stokes held the chairman of the State Board. Following the death of Albart Simon, the first general elder, in 1928. Stokes was presented with the opportunity to become the leader. He refused the request because of his age and remained in the general secretary's office for over twenty-five years. In 1944, Stokes was appointed the first General bishop. He split with the organization over the remarriage of presiding bishop Sidney Coy Bass in 1955.

Stokes, who held the charter of Incorporation, founded the Original Glorious Church of God in Christ along with Quander L. Wilson and Isaiah Hamiter. He served as chair of the West Virginia state board until he died in 1966.

Marshall Taylor 1928-2015

Marshall Taylor was a national evangelist who traveled and preached throughout the United States. Born in Brownsville, Tennessee, his family moved to Ypsilanti, Michigan. Taylor served briefly in the United States Army but later became involved in street crimes, resulting in his incarceration at Jackson State Prison for three years. After his release from prison, Taylor experienced the baptism of the Holy Spirit and acknowledged his call to the ministry.

He traveled throughout the United States following his ordination as an evangelist for PAW. In 1961, he became the pastor of Grace Apostolic Church in Ann Arbor, Michigan. Taylor gave up the pastorate in 1971 and returned to full-time evangelism. One of the great apostolic preachers, sermons such as "Roots I and Roots II" and "Praises Changes Things" were popular recordings within the movement. In 2015, Taylor was awarded PAW's Legacy Award for forty years as an evangelist.

Horace Temple 1889-1972

Way Back to Pentecost Church was the first Apostolic church established in Washington, DC. Sometime before 1916, G. T. Haywood sent Guy Jameson from Cleveland, Ohio, to DC to establish an Apostolic church in that city. Jameson also was the pastor of a church in Cleveland while he led the small storefront in DC. In 1930, Horace Temple, who served as a deacon, was ordained an elder and appointed pastor.

Born in King William County, Virginia, Temple created the name "Way Back to Pentecost" and financially supported the church during the Great Depression. He served as Treasurer of the DC, Delaware, Maryland District Council from 1941 to 1958. Temple was the pastor of Way Back to Pentecost for forty-two years.

Further Reading:
Noble, Earl M. *And They yet Speak: Historical Survey of African American Pentecostal-Holiness Churches in the Nation's Capital, Washington, D.C., 1900-2006.* Washington, D.C: Middle Atlantic Regional Press, 2007.

Robert Franklin Tobin 1894-1947

The leader of Pentecostal Assemblies of the World served as general secretary and pastored the "mother church" Christ Temple in Indianapolis, Indiana. Born in Elizabethtown, Kentucky, Tobin played for five years for the Negro National League. He served during World War I when the military first integrated blacks into the armed forces. Tobin moved to Indianapolis and attended Apostolic Faith Assembly upon returning from the war.

He was baptized in Jesus' name and ordained into the ministry in 1918. Several years later, he took over as pastor of the Apostolic Faith Church in Grand Rapids, Michigan. Tobin returned to Indianapolis in 1931 and was appointed pastor of Christ Temple after the death of G. T. Haywood. In addition, Tobin was appointed General Secretary of PAW. He also served as the first secretary of the Apostolic Bible Student Association. His sudden death shocked PAW and Christ Temple members, the church he had pastored for fifteen years.

Lambert Roosevelt Tolbert 1901-1948

Lambert R. Tolbert began attending Christ Temple in Indianapolis, Indiana, under the leadership of G. T. Haywood sometime in 1918. He later became the pastor of the Christ Temple in Marion, Indiana, and one of the Apostolic Bible Student Association leaders.

In 1936, Tolbert left Indiana and traveled to New Haven, Connecticut, where he became the pastor of Beulah Heights Church. As the leader of one of the largest Apostolic churches in Connecticut, Tolbert served as vice chairman of the Pentecostal Assemblies of the World's Connecticut District Council (CDC) in 1939. He led Beulah Heights and Connecticut council until he died in 1948.

Joseph Morsel Turpin 1887-1943
Ruth Beatrice Turpin

One of the five original bishops of Pentecostal Assemblies of the World and the founder of the First Apostolic Faith Church in Baltimore, Maryland, was born one of twelve children to John and Cora Turpin in Denton, Maryland. He moved to Baltimore in search of employment in 1906 and was introduced to the Holiness movement at the King's Apostle Holy Church organized by Mother Carrie V. Gurry.

Turpin opened a small mission with his close friends, George Morton and Samuel Watson. John W. Pitcher, who later served as the first chairman of the International Pentecostal Assemblies, ordained the men in 1916. He and Mother Ruth B. Turpin were baptized in Jesus' name after visiting Henry Prentiss at the Apostolic Faith Assembly in Philadelphia, Pennsylvania.

In 1917, Turpin organized the Apostolic Faith Church, the "first" Apostolic church in Maryland. He affiliated his congregation with PAW in 1918 and shortly after was elected to serve as one of the twenty-one field superintendents. PAW appointed him to the Board of Elders in 1919 and the Board of Presbyters in 1921.

Turpin was one of the founding fathers of the Eastern District Council (EDC) in 1919. Under his leadership, the EDC grew to include over 200 churches in Maryland, Washington, DC, Pennsylvania, New York, Connecticut, Massachusetts, and New Jersey. In 1925, after PAW adopted an episcopal form of government, he was one of the five elected bishops.

After the death of G. T. Haywood, Turpin left PAW to join the Pentecostal Assemblies of Jesus Christ in 1932. He later returned to the organization in 1934 and continued his work in the Eastern District Council, later renamed the DC., Delaware, and Maryland District Council. A few years before his death, Turpin consecrated James T. Morris, the founder of Highway Christian Church, to the office of bishop.

When many Apostolic leaders refused to fellowship with non-Pentecostal denominations and avoided social issues, Turpin was a member of the Interdenominational Ministers Alliance and active in social justice. For example, in 1933, he joined several prominent Baptist ministers in Annapolis, Maryland, to protest the lynching of African American George Armwood. When Turpin died at the age of fifty-six in 1943, First Apostolic Faith Church was one of the largest congregations in PAW.

Harrison Twyman 1920-1992

A native of Fairfax, Virginia, Harrison Twyman was one of the co-founding leaders of United Way of the Cross Churches of Christ of the Apostolic Faith. Twyman served in the United States Army during World War II from 1943 to 1946. After he returned from military service, he joined Bible Way Church in Washington, DC, under the pastorate of Smallwood E. Williams. Ordained an elder in the COOLJC, Twyman joined Williams in 1957 after forming the Bible Way Church of Our Lord Jesus Christ.

After sixteen years of service in Bible Way World Wide, Twyman joined Joseph H. Adams, former bishop of Way of the Cross, and James Pritchard, formerly of Apostle Church of Christ in God, to organize United Way of the Cross Churches of Christ. The organization he helped establish currently has fifty churches in North Carolina, South Carolina, Virginia, Maryland, New Jersey, Ohio, and the West Indies.

James Edison Tyson 1927-2011

Pentecostal Assemblies of the World bishop and pastor was born in Johnstown, Pennsylvania. Tyson joined the United States Navy during World War II at seventeen. After the war in 1946, he was baptized with the Holy Spirit in Youngstown, Ohio, under the leadership of Raymond L. Robinson. Called the ministry in 1947, Tyson joined PAW and served as Ohio District Council Youth Chairman.

He earned a Bachelor of Arts, Bachelor of Theology, and a master's degree from Indiana Christian University. After the death of his wife, Evelyn, Tyson met and married Betty Showell in 1981. Dr. Tyson-Showell served as president of Aenon Bible College and first lady of Christ Church Apostolic. In 1998, Tyson and his son in the Gospel, Norman L. Wagner, served as Presider and Assistant Presider of the PAW. During his tenure in PAW, his pastorate included Bethel Apostolic Church, Canton, Ohio; First Pentecostal Church, Leavenworth, Kansas; Mt. Calvary Pentecostal Church, Youngstown, Ohio; and Christ Temple "the Mother Church," Indianapolis, Indiana.

Betty Showell Tyson 1937-1996

Betty Showell Tyson was an Educator, Administrator, First Lady, and former President of Aenon Bible College. Betty was the oldest daughter of ten children born to Bishop Winfield A. and Mother Genevieve Showell. At First Apostolic Faith Church, where her father was pastor from 1944 to 1987, she served as Choir Director of the Echoneers Young Adult Choir for over twenty-five years. In addition, she was the director of the Vacation Bible School, Program Chairlady for the Women's Auxiliary, Editor of the Young People's Newsletter, and Young Adult Advisor.

Her father was one of the founding five bishops of Bible Way Church of Our Lord Jesus Christ World Wide in 1957. She was appointed the first secretary of Bible Way World Wide International Youth Congress by Bishop Smallwood E. Williams. As a member of the Bible Way organization, she organized the Bible Way "Little Folks" Convention and Junior Church.

Tyson was a distinguished scholar, school administrator, teacher, prolific writer, researcher, and educational consultant. She received a Bachelor of Science degree from Coppin State College and her Master of Arts from New York University. Her Ph.D. was earned and awarded at the University of Chicago.

In 1981, Betty married Bishop James E. Tyson, who pastored Christ Church Apostolic in Indianapolis. While serving as First Lady, Tyson was appointed president of Aenon Bible College in 1992. She implemented several new initiatives during her tenure, including the Pastors' Professional Development Program, the One Church-One Student Program, and the three hundred Student Recruitment Program. In addition, she revised the school's curriculum and established the *Circulus Scholarum* Honor Society. Dr. Tyson served as president of Aenon Bible College from 1992 to 1996.

Norman Leonard Wagner 1942-2010
Rita H. Wagner

The former presiding bishop of Pentecostal Assemblies of the World was born in Youngstown, Ohio and converted at the age of fourteen at Calvary Pentecostal Church under the leadership of Raymond L. Robinson. He acknowledged his call to the ministry at the age of twenty-three. Wagner graduated from Youngstown State University, where he later served as a lecturer, before earning bachelor's and master's degrees in theology from Aenon Bible College in Columbus and Indiana Bible College in Indianapolis.

Wagner took over as pastor of Calvary Pentecostal Church. Within a few years, the small congregation grew to a membership of 2,500 people, becoming one of the largest churches in Youngstown. Under his pastorate, the church established Calvary Christian Academy, the Saint's Saving and Trust Credit Union, and the Calvary Towers Senior Citizen Complex.

As a PAW member, Wagner served president as the National Young People's Union from 1973 to 1976 and bishop of the 13th Episcopal district that incorporated the state of Texas and the European Council of Nations, a network of forty churches throughout that continent. He was elected Assistant General Secretary and remained in that office until being elected presiding bishop of the organization in 1998, becoming one of the youngest presiding prelates in PAW history. He served in that position until 2004.

A pioneer in Black Gospel Television, he created a national weekly television program, "The Power of Pentecost," which aired on the Praise the Lord (PTL) and Armed Forces networks. In addition, Wagner was nominated with his choir for two Stellar Gospel Music Awards as a songwriter and singer. Wagner served on the Advisory committees for two White House administrations under President Ronald Reagan and President George W. Bush in the civic arena. In addition, he was named one of America's 100 outstanding black clergy members.

Charles Constantine Walsh
Christine Agatha Walsh

Charles and Christina Walsh were pioneers of the apostolic movement in Jamaica. Born in St. Mary, Jamaica, Christine was raised in the Baptist tradition and ordained Baptist minister. George White, a Pentecostal Assemblies of the World leader in Jamaican, introduced Christine and Charles to the Apostolic doctrine in 1936. Samuel J. Grimes, the presiding bishop of PAW, ordained the couple in 1939 but left PAW and founded Shiloh Apostolic Church in 1943.

Charles became the first Jamaican of African ancestry to hold the bishop's office and head a Pentecostal organization in Jamaica. He served as the presider of the organization from 1943 to 1967. Christine organized a church in St. Mary and several missions in Port Maria and Geddes Town. She was the first woman to be ordained a bishop in the Apostolic movement in Jamaica and served as president of Shiloh Apostolic Church from 1974 to 1975.

Charles William Watkins 1923-1988

Gospel singer, preacher, and pastor, Watkins was born in Richmond, Virginia. He was called to preach in 1945 and joined PAW. In 1954, he became the pastor of Lincoln Park Church of Christ in San Antonio. He left San Antonio to take over the pastorate of the Pentecostal Church of Christ in Cleveland, Ohio, in 1962. Within PAW, he served as the first National Minister of Music, president of the Young People's Union, and Diocesan of the Apostolic Student Bible Association Council. In 1973, he was consecrated as a bishop.

Watkins is best known as a gospel singer who sold over a million records. Gospel artists Rance Allen and Reverend James Cleveland recorded his songs. His rendition of *"I Won't Complain"* was popular among gospel singers. Some of his original compositions included "God is Great," "The Sound of Pentecost," and "Renew." Watkins was actively involved in the Civil Rights Movement. He invited Dr. Martin Luther King to his church to protest segregation and racism in Cleveland. Watkins also played a significant role in the election of Carl B. Stokes, the first black mayor in America, in 1967.

Robert Allen Wauls 1914-2016

Robert A. Wauls was born and educated in Gonzalez County, Texas. Raised in the Baptist faith, he encountered Pentecostalism and was called into the ministry in 1936. He traveled throughout Texas preaching on street corners following his call. Sometime after, Wauls established the "first" True Holiness Pentecostal Church in Altair, Texas, in 1937. He later founded four churches in San Antonio, Garwood, Fort Worth, and Wharton, Texas.

In 1966, he was elevated to the bishopric and served as leader of the 26th Episcopal District of Oklahoma from 1965 to 1971. PAW later assigned him as Bishop over the 13th Episcopal District of Texas, which he held for over twenty-four years. Finally, Wauls served as Bishop Emeritus until one hundred and two years old.

Joseph Weathers 1926-2010

The founder and first presiding prelate of Holy Temple Church of Christ was born in Sumter, South Carolina. He found employment at the Department of Agriculture in 1951 and retired from the federal government after twenty years of service. Weathers accepted the apostolic message in 1950 and joined the Way of the Cross Church of Christ under the pastorate of Henry C. Brooks. After Brooks' death, he appeared most likely to succeed as pastor. Instead, Weathers, Willie Davis, and Walter Thompson served as interim pastors on a four-month rotational basis.

In 1969, Presiding Bishop John L. Brooks assumed the pastorate of the church. When he did not receive the appointment, Weathers broke away with over one hundred members to form the Holy Temple Church of Christ. William L. Bonner consecrated him to the office of bishop in 1974. Years later, in 1979, he began the Holy Temple Church of Christ organization in Washington, DC. Weathers served as one of the leaders of the National Apostolic Fellowship. He presided over the Holy Temple Church of Christ for over thirty years.

Thomas John Weeks 1916-2013

Pentecostal Assemblies of the World statesman and bishop was born on the island of Montserrat, British West Indies. Moved by injustice during World War II, Weeks relocated to Canada and joined the allied armed forces. In 1942, after his discharge from the army, he traveled to America and resided in Boston, Massachusetts. Shortly after he arrived in the United States, he attended the Faithful Church of Christ and was baptized and filled with the Holy Spirit in 1942.

Weeks was called to the ministry and in 1958, he established Bethel Tabernacle Pentecostal Church and affiliated with the Massachusetts State Council. He was named Suffragan Bishop in 1966 and sent to the island of Barbados. In 1968, he was transferred from the Caribbean Council and placed over the Massachusetts State Council as the diocesan; he held this position for forty-one years.

Weeks studied at Northeastern University, Harvard University, Boston University, and Aenon Bible College. He founded several congregations in Massachusetts, including Bethel Tabernacle Pentecostal Church in Boston, Bethel Apostolic Church in Oaks Bluff, and Apostolic Faith Church in New Bedford. He also established the Bethel Apostolic Church and Emanuel Apostolic Church on the island of Montserrat. In 1994 Weeks resigned from the pastorate of Bethel Tabernacle. After his retirement, he served as the Eastern Caribbean Council of Nations chairman.

George White 1904-
Melvina E. Nelden White –1969

Born in the parish of St. Elizabeth, as a young man, George migrated to Kingston in the 1920s. He met and married Melvina E. Nelden in 1924. George affiliated with Pentecostal Assemblies of the World in 1925 and founded several churches throughout Kingston. PAW appointed him bishop over Jamaica in 1930 and he served as an editor of the *Christian Outlook*. In 1936, George founded the first congregation of the Union of Apostolic Churches. He migrated to Great Britain in 1938. Subsequently, during the 1940s, he traveled throughout the United States and England preaching the gospel.

Melvina was converted to Oneness Pentecostalism in 1919 and moved to Kingston in 1923 to work with Mother J. C. Russell, one of the early Oneness evangelists in Jamaica. Melvina planted over thirty churches in Jamaica, alone or with her husband. After her marriage to George, she confined her ministry to the West Indies. Melvina was instrumental in founding the Jamaica Union of Apostolic Churches, which became the Emmanuel Apostolic Church of Christ. In 1941, she convened the first convention of the Jamaica Union of Apostolic Churches. The organization became the first Jamaican organization to be incorporated in 1954.

Further Reading:

Gerloff, Roswith. *A Plea for British Black Theologies: The Black Church in Britain in its Transatlantic, Cultural and Theological Interaction with Special References to the Pentecostal Oneness (Apostolic) and Sabbatarian Movements.* Frankfurt am Maim: Peter Lang, 1992.

Frank W. Williams 1884-1932

Frank W. Williams was the first black Apostolic leader directly connected to the Azusa Street Revival and William J. Seymour. He attended the Bonnie Brae Street Prayer Meeting, where Seymour held his initial revival meetings before the Azusa Street building. Williams received the baptism of the Holy Spirit, and he took the Pentecostal message to the Deep South in Jackson, Mississippi, where he encountered Charles Harrison Mason, the founder of the Church of God in Christ.

His journey to Mississippi proved unsuccessful, so he relocated to Mobile, Alabama, where a revival occurred under his ministry. Among those converted was an entire congregation of the Primitive Baptist Church. The members gave Williams their building, and he named the church the Apostolic Faith Mission. Williams soon traveled throughout the South, establishing Pentecostal churches in Alabama, Florida, and Georgia. Saints Tabernacle in Birmingham became the headquarters for the organization.

During a tent revival in Birmingham, a young man named William T. Phillips heard the preaching of Williams. He embraced Pentecostalism and was ordained in 1913. Phillips later established Apostolic Overcoming Holy Church. Williams converted to Oneness Pentecostalism in 1915 and incorporated his organization under the name Apostolic Faith Mission Church of God. He led his organization for twenty-six years until his death in 1932.

Joseph David Williams, Sr. 1892-1966

Joseph D. Williams founded the Progressive Church of the Lord Jesus Christ. He initially organized the Pilgrim Church of Christ in Cleveland, Ohio, under the Church of Our Lord Jesus Christ of the Apostolic Faith. While visiting his family in the South, Williams was instrumental in the miraculous divine healing of his wife's niece, who had been diagnosed with terminal cancer. As a result, he resigned from his pastorate in Cleveland and relocated to Columbia, South Carolina, in 1944. Soon after, Williams incorporated his church under the Progressive Church of Our Lord Jesus Christ and served as the presiding bishop for twenty-two years. His organization has twenty-three churches and missions in North and South Carolina, Florida, Georgia, New York, and Africa.

Roy Constantine Williams 1929-2010

The Founder and first presiding bishop of the Church of Jesus Christ (Apostolic) was born in Camaguey, Cuba. When he was three years old, his family migrated to Jamaica, West Indies. Williams was baptized within the Catholic tradition in Cuba, yet later in 1946, he received the baptism of the Holy Spirit. At twenty, he was ordained to the ministry and began traveling throughout Jamaica preaching. In 1962, he settled in the United States in Paterson, New Jersey, where he established the Church of Jesus Christ Apostolic. Williams was consecrated to the office of apostle in 1993.

Williams attended Kingston Technical, and St. Simon College in Jamaica. He also holds a Certificate from the American Association of Christian Counselors, Center for Biblical Counseling in Forest, Virginia, a Master of Biblical Studies from the Institute of American Bible, and a Doctor of Philosophy from Kingdom Bible College in Fort Worth, Texas. His organization grew from a single congregation to churches in Canada, England, Africa, India, Jamaica, and United States.

McKinley Williams 1901-1981

One of the founding fathers of Bible Way Church of Our Lord Jesus Christ World Wide and early Apostolic leader in Philadelphia, was born in Sumter County, Georgia. He moved to Philadelphia, Pennsylvania, in 1920 and shortly after was baptized in the name of Jesus and received the baptism of the Holy Spirit. Williams joined Sherrod C. Johnson, who served as Overseer of the state of Pennsylvania in the Church of Christ of the Apostolic Faith under the leadership of Robert C. Lawson.

He served as a deacon but was later ordained an elder. Shortly after his ordination, Williams began preaching on street corners in South Philadelphia. In 1928, he founded the Refuge Church of Christ. While still pastoring in Philadelphia, Lawson sent him to Southern Pines, North Carolina, to organize a church and supervise the R. C. Lawson Institute.

In 1940, Williams started a radio broadcast heard every Sunday afternoon. He was a pioneer in religious broadcasting and one of the first Apostolic ministers in Philadelphia to have his weekly television program broadcast on WTAF-TV on channel 29. With his successful radio and television broadcast, membership of Refuge Church of Christ increased, and the church purchased a larger building in South Philadelphia.

Williams earned a Master's and Doctor of Theology degree from American Bible College in Chicago, Illinois, in 1953. He also attended Temple University and received an honorary degree of Doctor of Divinity from American Bible College. In 1957, he was consecrated as one of the five founding bishops of the Bible Way World Wide. Regarded by many as a strict disciplinarian, Williams served as Diocesan over Pennsylvania and Georgia. He also established churches in Nigeria, West Africa, and the Virgin Islands.

Like Smallwood E. Williams, he addressed social issues in the black community. In 1961, Williams joined many black pastors of Philadelphia in their protest of the Gulf Oil Company, which refused to hire black workers. Williams urged his congregation to boycott the company until it changed its hiring practices. He served as Vice Presiding Bishop of Bible Way and pastor of Refuge Church of Christ for twenty-four years.

Further Reading:
"Bishop William McKinley," Bible Way News Voice, December 1981.

Smallwood Edmond Williams 1907-1991
Verna Lucille Williams 1907-2000

The founder of Bible Way Church of Our Lord Jesus Christ World Wide and Civil Rights activist was born in Lynchburg, Virginia. His family migrated to Columbus, Ohio, in 1917 to escape segregation in the South. While in Columbus, his mother, Mary Wilson, joined the Church of Christ of the Apostolic Faith, pastored by Robert C. Lawson in 1919. A few months after Mother Wilson joined the church, Lawson moved to Harlem, New York and Karl F. Smith served as pastor in the absence of Lawson.

In March 1919, Williams' life forever changed at age twelve when he was filled with the Holy Ghost and baptized in Jesus' name. Following his conversion, Williams received his call to the ministry at fourteen and was ordained at the age of eighteen in 1925. Known as the "boy preacher," he traveled and preached throughout New York, Chicago, Columbus, St. Louis, Philadelphia, and Boston.

In 1927, at the request of Lawson, Williams traveled to Washington, DC, to organize a church. Upon his arrival in DC, he began preaching next to a fire hydrant on a street corner. While establishing his ministry in 1928, Williams married Verna L. Rapley, a piano teacher who was a member of the Refuge Church of Christ in New York. His street preaching allowed him to build a congregation, first holding services in an old theater building. Then, in 1936, the membership moved into a new edifice. By 1947, the congregation was able to build a 3,000-seat building.

Williams worked closely with Lawson in his organization for over thirty-eight years, first serving as President of the Sunday School Association, then as treasurer, and as General Secretary for twenty years. In 1957, he split with COOLJC over Lawson's autocratic leadership style. As a result, the Bible Way Church of Our Lord Jesus Christ World Wide was born out of the National Pentecostal Ministerial Conference. At this conference, Williams, John S. Beane, Winfield A. Showell, Joseph Moore, and McKinley Williams were consecrated as the founding bishop of Bible Way World Wide.

For many years, Williams was at the forefront of the fight against racial inequality and injustice, specifically in the District of Columbia. In 1952, years before the historic Brown vs. the Board of Education Supreme Court decision, he conducted a one-day sit-in with his six-year-old son, Wallace Williams, at an "all-white" school in the city. Williams believed Wallace should attend the "best" school nearest to their home rather than an overcrowded school several miles away. His staged sit-in brought citywide attention to the unequal education of the black community.

As a force in politics for many years, he served as President of the DC chapter of the Southern Christian Leadership Conference and as a delegate for the National Convention of the Democratic Party. In 1968, he began construction on the Golden Rule Housing Complex, a housing development for low-income families. The apartments consisted of 184 high-rise units, complete with air conditioning, balconies, laundry facilities, a playground, and a daycare facility.

A progressive leader, he worked alongside non-Pentecostal leaders. During the 1950s, he served as President of the Ministers Alliance of Washington DC. The Interdenominational Ministers Alliance was an organization comprised of more than a hundred ministers from various denominations. He was also a member of the Interfaith Council of Religions (ICR). Williams was a progressive leader who worked alongside non-Pentecostal leaders. During the 1950s, he served as President of the Interdenominational Ministers Alliance and was a member of the Interfaith Council of Religions (ICR), a coalition of Catholic, Protestant, and Jewish leaders.

Williams' lasting goal was to unify the black apostolic movement. His dream of unity was realized in 1963 when he brought together one hundred Pentecostal leaders. From this historic meeting, the Apostolic Inter-organizational Fellowship Conference was born. The AIFC held conferences from 1963 to 1991 but disbanded after the death of Williams.

Under his leadership and guidance, Bible Way Church of Our Lord Jesus Christ became one of the most recognizable black Apostolic organizations with 250,000 members and 350 churches throughout America, Africa, Jamaica, and England.

Further Reading:
Williams, Smallwood Edmond. *This Is My Story: A Significant Life Struggle : Autobiography of Smallwood Edmond Williams.* Washington, D.C.: Wm. Willoughby Publishers, 1981.

⎯⎯⎯⎯. Brief History and Doctrine of the Bible Way Churches of Our Lord Jesus Christ World Wide. Washington, D.C.: The Church, 1957.

Quander Lear Wilson 1918-2003

The founder and first presiding bishop of the Greater Emmanuel Apostolic Churches was born in Berwyn, Pennsylvania, and educated in Philadelphia. Wilson preached his initial sermon in 1937, became a licensed minister in 1940, and was ordained an elder the following year. His first pastorate was in Philadelphia after he relocated to Oberlin, Ohio, to pastor, Glorious Faith Tabernacle after the departure of Isaiah W. Hamiter in 1950. Wilson held the position of General Secretary from 1953 until 1955 in the Glorious Church of God in Christ. He attended Crozier Bible Institute and Chester Theological Seminary in Chester, Pennsylvania, and received his Ph.D. from the Florida State Christian College in Fort Lauderdale, Florida, in 1971.

In 1955, Wilson split with his parent organization and joined the Original Glorious Church of God in Christ with W. O. Howard, Cleveland H. Stokes, and Isaiah Hamiter. In 1960, he left Original Glorious Church and founded Greater Emmanuel Apostolic Faith Tabernacle, Inc. The organization initially began with three churches. Under the leadership of Wilson, Greater Emmanuel grew to include several churches throughout the United States and Africa. In addition, Wilson mentored and was a "spiritual father" to many well-known pastors and ministers. Notably, nationally known preacher and pastor T. D. Jakes joined the Greater Emmanuel Gospel Tabernacle in Charleston, West Virginia, and was ordained as a bishop by Wilson in 1987. In 2000, because of failing health he resigned as presiding bishop, turning over the position to Bishop Edward E. Shouse.

Elzie William Young 1913-1989

The longest-serving bishop of Pentecostal Churches of the Apostolic Faith was born in Lexington, Kentucky. Elzie was baptized in Jesus' name at the age of eight at the First Pentecostal Church in Lexington. He later received the baptism of the Holy Spirit in 1932 at the age of nineteen. For a short time, Young worked as a professional jockey but was unable to maintain his weight.

He acknowledged his call to the ministry and traveled as an evangelist across the country. In 1950, he affiliated with Pentecostal Assemblies of the World and founded Greater Bethlehem Temple Apostolic Church in Cincinnati, Ohio. Young left PAW and joined Pentecostal Churches of the Apostolic Faith organized by Samuel N. Hancock in 1957.

Within PCAF, he served as District Elder of Ohio and was appointed to the office of bishop in 1958. Young held the office of Assistant Presiding Bishop under the administration of Willie Lee. He was elected as the presiding bishop after the departure of Lee in 1964. During his tenure, PCAF grew to a net worth of

$1,000,000.00. Young was presiding prelate for twenty-five years and the only PCAF presider unanimously re-elected to serve a life term.

Representative Black Oneness Organizations

Organizations	Est	Founder(s)	Parent Body
Church of God (Apostolic)		Thomas J. Cox	
Pentecostal Assemblies of the World	1906		
Apostolic Faith Mission Church of God	1906	Frank W. Williams	Apostolic Faith Mission (Seymour)
Apostolic Overcoming Holy Church of God	1916	Williams T. Phillips	Apostolic Faith Mission Church of God
Emmanuel Tabernacle Baptist Church of the Apostolic Faith	1916	Martin R. Gregory	
Church of Our Lord Jesus Christ of the Apostolic Faith	1919	Robert C. Lawson	Pentecostal Assemblies of the World
Glorious Church of God in Christ	1921	Cleveland H. Stokes Lulu Phillips	Triumph the Church and Kingdom of God in Christ
New Pentecostal Church of God in Christ	1925	A D. Bradley Lonnie Bates	Church of God in Christ
The Churches of God and True Holiness	1927	John W. Garlington	
Way of the Cross Church of Christ	1933	Henry C. Brooks	Church of Our Lord Jesus Christ
Church of The Lord Jesus Christ of the Apostolic Faith	1933	Sherrod C. Johnson	Church of Our Lord Jesus Christ
Zion Gospel Churches of the Apostolic Faith	1938	J. P. Shields	Church of Our Lord Jesus Christ
Highway Christian Church of Christ	1941	James T. Morris	Pentecostal Assemblies of the World
Apostle Church of Christ in God	1941	J. W. Ardrey James C. Richardson J. Jenkins W. R. Bryant M Williams	Church of God (Apostolic)
Progressive Church of Our Lord Jesus Christ, Inc.	1944	Joseph D. Williams	Church of Our Lord Jesus Christ
Church of God in Jesus Christ (Apostolic)	1946	Randolph A. Carr	Church of God In Christ

Organizations	Est	Founder(s)	Parent Body
Original Glorious Church of God in Christ	1955	W. O. Howard	Glorious Church of God in Christ
Highway Churches of Christ	1955	Raymond F. Davis	Highway Christian Church of Christ
Pentecostal Churches of the Apostolic Faith	1957	Samuel N. Hancock	Pentecostal Assemblies of the World
Bible Way Church of Our Lord Jesus Christ World Wide	1957	Smallwood E. Williams	Church of Our Lord Jesus Christ
Bible Way Pentecostal Apostolic Church	1960	Curtis Jones	Church of Our Lord Jesus Christ
Holy Temple Church of the Lord Jesus Christ	1961	Randolph Goodwin	Church of The Lord Jesus Christ
True Vine Pentecostal Churches of Jesus	1961	Robert L. Hairston	True Vine Pentecostal Holiness Churches
Free Gospel Churches of the Apostles' Doctrine	1962	Ralph E. Green	Way of the Cross Church of Christ
Apostolic Inter-Organizational Fellowship Conference	1963	Smallwood E. Williams	Bible Way Church of Our Lord Jesus Christ
Living Witness of the Apostolic Faith	1963	Charles Poole Mattie Poole	Pentecostal Churches of the Apostolic Faith
Mount Hebron Apostolic Temple of Our Lord Jesus Christ	1963	George H. Wiley	Apostle Church of Christ in God
Emmanuel Pentecostal Church of Our Lord	1964	Willie Lee	Pentecostal Churches of the Apostolic Faith
	1965	Monroe R. Saunders	Church of God in Jesus Christ (Apostolic)
Cainhoy Miracle Revival Corporation	1969	Helen Smith	Church of Our Lord Jesus Christ
Apostolic Assemblies of Christ	1970	George M. Boone	Pentecostal Churches of the Apostolic Faith
United Churches of Jesus, Apostolic	1970	J. W. Ardrey	Apostle Church of Christ in God
Refuge Temple Assembly of Yahweh	1970	John W. Pernell	Church of The Lord Jesus Christ
Church of Jesus Christ Apostolic, Inc	1971	Roy C. Williams	

Organizations	Est	Founder(s)	Parent Body
Evangelistic Churches of Christ of the Apostolic Faith	1974	Lymus L. Johnson	Church of Our Lord Jesus Christ
United Way of the Cross of the Apostolic Faith	1974	Joseph Adams, Harrison J. Twyman, James Pritchard	Way of the Cross Church of Christ
Alliance of Apostolic Churches of Christ Jesus	1977	Albert E. Dixon	Churches of God and True Holiness
Holy Temple Church of Christ	1979	Joseph E. Weather	Way of the Cross Church of Christ
Redeemed Assembly of Jesus Christ, Apostolic	1979	James F. Harris	Highway Christian Church of Christ
Higher Ground Always Abounding Assemblies	1988	Sherman S. Watkins	
Beth-El Churches of Christ	1989	Robert Evans	Highway Churches of Christ
World Assemblies of Restoration	1995	James Nelson	Pentecostal Assemblies of the World
Apostolic Faith Fellowship International	2012	Charles Johnson	Pentecostal Assemblies of the World

Historic Events in the Black Apostolic Movement

1906	The outpouring of the Holy Spirit begins at the Azusa Street Revival in Los Angeles, California under William J. Seymour
1906	Henry Prentiss visits Azusa Street Revival Pentecostal Assemblies of the World established
1910	Garfield Thomas (G. T.) Haywood becomes pastor of Apostolic Faith Assembly (later renamed Christ Temple)
1913	Worldwide Camp meeting at Arroyo Seco, California. Robert A. McAlister preaches baptism in the name of Jesus
1915	Haywood baptized in the name of Jesus Pentecostal Assemblies of the World embraces Oneness Pentecostalism
1916	William Phillips established Ethiopian Overcoming Holy Church
1919	Robert C. Lawson established the Church of Christ of the Apostolic Faith
1925	Haywood elected the first presiding bishop and Joseph M. Turpin, A. R. Schooler, G. B. Rowe, and A. F. Varnell appointed bishops of PAW
1931	Haywood dies Church of Christ of the Apostolic Faith is renamed Church of Our Lord Jesus Christ
1941	Ethiopian Overcoming Holy Church is renamed Apostolic Overcoming Holy Church
1957	Smallwood E. Williams establishes Bible Way Church of Our Lord Jesus World Wide Samuel Hancock founds Pentecostal Churches of the Apostolic Faith
1961	Robert C. Lawson and Sherrod C. Johnson die
1963	Williams organizes Pentecostal Leadership Conference
1969	Helen Smith establishes Cainhoy Revival Center as first woman to establish an organization out of the Church of Our Lord Jesus Christ
1989	William L. Bonner and Smallwood Williams hold Pentecostal Apostolic Fellowship Crusade at Meadowlands, New Jersey
1991	Smallwood E. Williams dies
2006	Azusa Street Revival celebrates Centennial
2015	Black Apostolic movement celebrates Centennial Althea J. Cushionberry consecrated first woman PAW bishop
2016	Bonnie Hunter consecrated first woman bishop in International Bible Church of Jesus Christ

Further Readings

A Short History of Bethel United Church of Jesus Christ Apostolic. London, England: Bethel United Church of Jesus Christ Apostolic, 2019.

Blumhofer, Edith L. *Pentecost in My Soul: Explorations in the Meaning of Pentecostal Experience in the Early Assemblies of God.* Springfield, MO: Gospel Publishing, 1989.

Bonner, Ethel. *This is My Story.* Unpublished manuscript.

Brazier, Arthur M, Larry Crowe, and Matthew Hickey. The Historymakers Video Oral History with Bishop Arthur Brazier, 2016.

Burton, Michael C. *Deep Roots: The African/Black Contribution to Christianity: A Study of the African/Black Personalities of the Bible, African/Black Church Fathers and the Major Contributions of the Early Black Church to Christianity,* Bloomington, IN: IUniverse Inc, 2008.

D. C., Delaware, and Maryland District Council, 50ᵀᴴ Jubilee Year 1937-1987. n.p.: Pentecostals Assemblies of the World, n.d.

Dargan, William Thomas, and Kathy White Bullock. "Willie Mae Ford Smith of St. Louis: A Shaping Influence upon Black Gospel Singing Style." *Black Music Research Journal* 9.2 (1989) 249–70.

Discipline and Manuel of Church of God Apostolic. Winston-Salem, NC: Church of God (Apostolic), n.p., n.d.

Dortch, Sammie M. *When God Calls: A Biography of Bishop Arthur M. Brazier.* Grand Rapids, MI: W.B. Eerdmans, 1996.

DuPree, Sherry Sherrod. *Biographical Dictionary of African American Holiness-Pentecostal 1880-1990.* Washington: Mid-Atlanta Regional, 1989.

Fairley, David L. *Moved by Such a Man.* Muncie, IN: n.p., 1980.

Garrett Gary W. and Nathaniel A. Urshan. *The Life and Times of Bishop Morris E. Golder.* Eureka, IL: Apostolic Christian, 2000.

Gerloff, Roswith. *A Plea for British Black Theologies: The Black Church in Britain in its Transatlantic, Cultural and Theological Interaction with Special*

References to the Pentecostal Oneness (Apostolic) and Sabbatarian Movements. Frankfurt am Maim: Peter Lang, 1992.

Golder, Morris E. *The History of the Pentecostal Assemblies of the World.* Indianapolis: n.p., 1973.

_____. *The Bishops of the Pentecostal Assemblies of the World,* Indianapolis, IN: s.n., 1980.

_____. *The Life and Works of Bishop Garfield Thomas Haywood (1880-1931).* Indianapolis, IN: s.n., 1977.

Haywood, G. T., and Paul D. Dugas. *The Life and Writings of Elder G. T. Haywood.* Portland, OR: Apostolic Book Publishers, 1968.

Holy Church of God, Inc., and Its Founder: Including "What We Believe." Birmingham, AL: Forniss, 1984.

Hyatt, Eddie L. *Fire on the Earth: Eyewitness Reports from the Azusa Street Revival.* Lake Mary: Creation House, 2006.

Johnson, Fitz G. *Born for a Purpose: The Autobiography of Sydney Alexander Dunn.* S.l.: Grosvenor House Publishing Ltd. 2016.

Johnson, Margaret G. *My Call to Africa.* n.p.: n.p., n.d.

LeBlanc, Deborah Sims. *Like a Rose ...: Life, Times, and Messages of the Late Bishop Frank R. Bowdan, D.D. 1910-1976.* Los Angeles, CA: DLB Associates, 1989.

McEady, Vivian. "History of the Founder: Biography of Bishop Sherrod C. Johnson, 1919–1950." The Church of the Lord Jesus Christ of the Apostolic Faith. Online: http://www.apostolicministries.net/late_bishop_johnson.htm.

Minute Book and Ministerial Record of the Pentecostal Assemblies of the World (Indianapolis: Pentecostal Assemblies of the World, 1918-1919).

Noble, Earl M. *And They yet Speak: Historical Survey of African American Pentecostal-Holiness Churches in the Nation's Capital, Washington, D.C., 1900-2006.* Washington, D.C: Middle Atlantic Regional Press, 2007.

Payne, Leonard M. Jr. *My People Yesterday, Today and Forever: A History of the Glorious Church of God in Christ.* n.i.: Xlibris, 2008, 86.

Pentecostal Assemblies of the World. *The Christian Outlook Magazine.* Indianapolis, IN: Pentecostal Assemblies of the World, 1929.

_____. *The Christian Outlook Magazine.* Indianapolis, IN: Pentecostal Assemblies of the World, 1933.

Reeder, Hilda. *A Brief History of the Foreign Missionary Department of the Pentecostal Assemblies of the World.* Indianapolis: Foreign Missionary Dept, 1951.

Richardson, James C. *God's Chosen Prelate: The Life and Ministry of Bishop James C. Richardson, Sr.* Capital Heights, MD: Seymour Press, 2019.

_____. With Water and Spirit: A History of Black Apostolic Denominations in the U.S. Washington DC: Spirit, 1980.

Rose, Sylvia. *The life of Mother Sylvia Rose,* n.p:, n.d.

Rules and By-Laws of the Church of the Lord Jesus Christ of the Apostolic Faith. Philadelphia, PA: Church of the Lord Jesus Christ, 1944.

Russell, J. C. "A Brief History of the United Pentecostal Church in Jamaica" *The Evening Light.* August 1986.

Saunders, Monroe R. *Sermons and Hymns from My Heart.* Enumclaw, WA: Pleasant Word, 2004.

Sims, Jane A. *Telling Our Story: The Role and Contributions of Women, Particularly Women of Color, in the Formation of the Pentecostal/Holiness Movement and the Pentecostal Assemblies of the World.* 2002.

Smith, Aaron J. *A Devout Man: Biography of Karl F. Smith, 1892-1972.* Atlanta, GA: JacLyn Enterprises, 1998.

Smith, Helen. *You're Going to Be Somebody.* Mobile, AL: Gazelle, 1999.

Stewart, Alexander C, and Sherry S. DuPree. *The Silent Spokesman: Bishop Robert Clarence Lawson, Founder of the Church of Our Lord Jesus Christ of the Apostolic Faith, Inc.*, New York City. Gainesville, Fla: Displays for Schools, 1994.

Taylor, Clarence. *The Black Churches of Brooklyn.* New York: Columbia University Press, 1994.

Tucker, Anjulet. "Apostolic Faith Mission Church of God." *In African American Religious Cultures*, edited by Stephen C. Finley and Torin Alexander, 88–90. Santa Barbara, CA: ABC-CLIO, 2009.

Tyson, J. Laverne. *A Definitive History of the Pentecostal Assemblies of the World: A Narrative & Pictorial Study in 7 Volumes:* Volume 1, 1914–1930, Indianapolis: Tyson, 1998.

W. L. Bonner Literary Committee. *And the High Places I'll Bring Down: Bishop William L. Bonner, the Man and His God.* Detroit, MI: W. L. Bonner Literary Committee, 1999.

Wallace, Mary H. Profiles of Pentecostal Missionaries. Hazelwood: Word Aflame press, 1986.

Walters, Steve B. *A Shepherd's Journey: The Life Story of Apostle Lymus L. Johnson.* n.p.: Steve Walters Ministries, 2002.

Williams, Pandora. *Outstanding Women and their Contributions to the Church of Our Lord Jesus Christ of the Apostolic Faith*, Inc. S.l.: International Missionary Department, 1994.

Williams, Shirley and Samuel McDowell Shelton. *Blessedness, the Greatest Miracle in My Life!: His Holy Apostolic Blessedness: A Man After God's Own Heart!* S.l: S. Wms Enterprises LLC, 2014.

Williams, Smallwood Edmond. *Brief History and Doctrine of the Bible Way Churches of Our Lord Jesus Christ World Wide.* Washington, D.C.: The Church, 1957.

_____. *This Is My Story: A Significant Life Struggle: Autobiography of Smallwood Edmond Williams.* Washington, D.C.: Wm. Willoughby Publishers, 1981.

Index of Names

Abney, William Charles, 75-76
Abney, Elaine, 76
Adams, Joseph H., 29, 63, 77-78, 273
Akers, Elmer Fremont, 39, 79
Ali, Muhammad, 33
Allen, Rance, 280
Ardrey, J. W., 35, 63, 80, 132
Ayers, George Washington, 18, 81-82, 236
Ayers, Verley Mildred, 81, 82

Barber, Odduous, 8, 83, 165
Barnes, John, D., 84
Barnes, Rosa, 84
Barnes, William Samuel, Jr., 40
Barnes, William Samuel, Sr., 39, 40, 85, 114
Bass, Ralph, 86
Bass, Sidney Coy, 25, 86, 161
Beane, John Solomon, 46, 88, 169, 255
Beane, Miranda, 88
Bell, D. Rayford, 44, 45, 89
Bollinger, Catherine, 90
Bollinger, Isaiah W., 90, 93
Bonner, Ethel Mae, 91-92, 93
Bonner, William Lee, 23, 53, 66, 90, 91, 93-94, 174, 282
Boone, George Marshall, 59, 95-96
Boone, Mae Dee, 95
Bowdan, Frank Reuben, 53, 97-99, 176, 177
Bowdan, Maggie, 97, 99, 134
Bowdan, William S., 97, 99
Bowers, Paul Alexander, 11, 100

Bragg, Bernard Nathaniel, 70, 101-02
Brazier, Arthur Monroe, 103-104
Brazier, Byron T., 104
Brazier, Geneva, 103
Brazier, Isabelle, 103
Brisbin, Lawrence E., 11
Bryant, W. R., 14, 80
Bridges, Norman D., 84
Bridges, Peter F., 39, 105-06, 198
Brooks, Alphonzo D., 30, 67, 141
Brooks, George Harold, 11, 107-08
Brooks, Henry Chauncey, 22, 29, 77, 109-110, 111, 282
Brooks, Isabell, 141
Brooks, John Luke, 29, 66, 111, 139, 282
Brooks, Laura, 111
Brooks, Nellie, 107
Brooks, Theodore L., 11, 108
Brooks, Willie Shaw, 109, 141
Brown, Donice, 15
Brown, Henry H., 112, 113
Brown, Minnie, 112, 113
Bush, George W., 278
Butler, Ramsey Nathaniel, 71, 84, 113

Cage, Byron, 75
Calloway, Lucille Tanzella, 114
Campbell, Lawreance G., 47, 48
Cannady, Leroy H., 30, 139
Carr, Randolph Adolphus, 39, 57, 79, 85, 106, 115-16, 243
Carmichael, Stockley, 33
Carson, William A., 97, 117, 135
Chenault, Dunlap, 8, 118, 188

311

Clark, H. C., 20
Clark, James I., Jr., 23, 120
Clark, James I., Sr., 21, 119-120
Cleaver, Eldredge, 33
Cleveland, James, 280
Collins, David, 10, 121, 161
Colston, Azel C., 26
Cook, Glen A., 2, 7, 160, 165, 225
Cooke, George, 8, 122
Cooper, Bramlett, 59
Cox, Thomas J., 13, 35, 80, 123, 135, 188, 209
Crawford, Florence, 7, 225
Crossley, William, 124
Cushinberry, Aletha June, 11, 125

Dampier, F. C., 20
Davis, Belle, 126, 127, 187
Davis, Hebert John, 8, 127
Davis, Raymond Fox, 34, 43, 69, 128
Davis, Riley Marcilous, 129-30
Dixon, Albert E., 27, 65
Dixon, Nah William, 131
Dockett, Bessie, 19, 153
Dorsey, Thomas, 261
Doub, Robert Oliver, 35, 67, 132, 152
Douglas, Anne Belle Davis, 133-34, 161
Douglas, Floyd Ignatius, 8, 97, 117, 134-35, 166, 248
Draft, Johnnie, 14, 60
Dunn, Sydney Alexander, 39, 57, 137-38

Eggleston, Harry Clay, 29, 139
Ellis, Charles H., 11, 125, 206
Evans, Robert, 43, 69, 140
Ewart, Frank, 2, 97, 163

Faison, Raymond, 27, 65
Faison, William J., 40
Ford, Isabell Brooks, 141
Ford, Lillian, 142
Franklin, James O., 199
Frazee, J. J., 7, 8, 166

Garlington, John Wesley, Jr., 27, 143-44
Garlington, John Wesley, Sr., 27, 143, 145
Garvey, Marcus, 17, 219, 221
Gates, Lambert W., 44, 205
Gerald, William, 146
Golder, Morris Ellis., 147-48,
Goode, Benjamin J., 75, 149
Goodwin, Randolph, 32, 56, 150
Goss. Howard, 8
Grant, Lela, 19, 153
Grant, Simon Tenyen, 151
Green, Belton, 56
Green, Ralph E., 52, 67, 152
Green, Shirley M., 52, 152
Gregory, Martin Rawleigh., 19, 25, 153-54, 204, 220
Grimes, Samuel Joshua., 10, 44, 79, 107, 136, 148, 155-56, 172, 248, 260
Grimes, Sobrina Kathleen, 156, 157-58, 171
Groover, Gentle, 23, 94
Gurry, Carrie V., 271

Hamiter, Isaiah Warren, 41, 159, 266, 297
Hancock, Samuel Nathaniel, 8, 9, 10, 44, 44, 84, 95, 97, 117, 121, 160-61, 256
Harewood, Gladstone Thomas, 162
Harewood, Richard, 162

Harris, James Frank, 34, 66
Harris, Thoro, 163-6
Haywood, Garfield, Thomas, 2, 7, 8, 9, 21, 83, 105, 122, 133, 147, 162, 165-67, 168, 231, 241, 268
Haywood, Ida, 161, 165, 168
Holly, John Silas, 9, 46, 53, 162, 169-70, 212, 246
Holmes, Aaron, 170, 181
Holmes, Pearl, 170, 181
Hopkins, Moore Ellen, 156, 157, 171
Hopkins (Sister), 7
Howard, W. O., 25, 41, 172
Hunter, Bonnie, 48
Hunter, Lenist J., 173
Hutner, Maurice H., 23, 93, 174, 215, 264
Hutner, Ruth, 174

Jackson, Frank, 27
Jackson, Lulu, 175
Jackson, Jesse, 143
Jackson, Mahalia, 261
Jackson, Sylvester Norma, 176
Jakes, T. D., 50, 68, 298
Jenkins, Jerome J., 14, 35, 80
Jennings, Gino, 32
Johnson, Charles, 71
Johnson, James Archie, 11, 177-78
Johnson, Lymus Leewood, 23, 53, 63, 179-80
Johnson, Maragret Giles, 181-82
Johnson, Sherrod Charlotte, 21, 22, 31, 56, 150, 173, 179, 183-184, 291
Jones, Curtis P., 49
Jones, Henry, 215
Jones, O. T., 115

Jones Pearl Williams, 185-86

King, Martin Luther, 104, 143, 189, 280

Lawson, Carrie, 126, 187, 189
Lawson, Robert Clarence, 8, 13, 19, 21, 22, 23, 29, 31, 47, 88, 93, 118, 122, 126, 153, 187-90, 191, 207, 250, 259, 293
Layne, Austin Augustus, 9, 191-92, 198
Layne, Austin Samuel, 193
Leaston, Heardie, 10, 44, 121, 195
Lee, Clester Richard, 194
Lee, Willie, 10, 44, 195
Levant, George Grover, 196
Lightford Susan Gertrude, 8, 115, 191, 197-98, 226
Lomax, J. V., 34, 53, 66

Mason, Charles H., 39, 115, 287
Mason, Lillian, 199
Matthews, John H., 18
McAlister, Robert A., 2
McGoings, Robert James, 200
McMurray, Robert William, 201-202
McPherson, Aimee Semple, 163
Miller, Marion B., 203, 250
Mills, Mary E., 204
Mitchell, Edward M., 20
Moody, Dwight L., 164
Moore, Benjamin Thomas, 205
Moore, Clarence E., 206
Moore, Dora Belle, 206
Moore, Herbert C., 103
Moore, J. E., 45
Moore, Joseph, 46, 47, 207

Morris, James Thomas, 34, 43, 110, 113, 128, 254, 272

Neal, E. N., 13, 14, 35, 49, 123, 209
Nelson, Floyd Edward, 48, 65, 210-11
Nelson, James D., 70
Nelson, Yvonne, 210, 211

Paddock, Ross, 10, 98, 257
Parchia, Earl, 212
Parham, Charles Fox, 1
Parrott, James Walter, 213
Paulceus, Joseph, 214
Pender, Richard J., 69
Pernell, John W., 23, 53, 61, 215, 263
Perry, Delphia, 22, 216
Perry, Lindsey, 26
Pettiford, Beverly D., 217, 218
Pettiford, Emma Heil, 217, 218
Pettiford, Odell Greer, 218
Pettiford, Otho, 225, 218
Phillips, Lulu, 17, 19, 25, 87, 153, 219-220
Phillips, William Thomas, 17, 18, 221-222, 288
Pitcher, John W., 271
Poole, Charles Edward, 54, 223, 224
Poole, Mattie Bell, 54, 223-224
Powell, Adam Clayton, 189, 197
Pratt, Ann Story, 11
Prentiss, Henry, 31, 83, 122, 165, 183, 225-26, 271
Pritchard, James, 63, 77, 273
Pryor, Hattie Edwards, 227

Randolph, A. Phillip, 129, 189
Reagan, Ronald, 278

Redd, Lucy, 233
Redd, Viola, 228
Reed, Jeremiah, 229-230
Reed, Willie Mae, 229, 230
Reeder, Hilda, 9, 231-232
Reid, Cecil O., 14
Reide, Mona, 11
Richardson, James C. Jr., 36
Richardson, James C. Sr., 14, 35, 60, 233-34
Robinson, Carey, 119
Robinson, Raymond L., 274, 277
Roby, Jasper, 18, 82, 235-236
Rogers, Huie L., 47, 207
Rookard, Willie, 48
Rose, Sylvia, 237-38
Rowe, G. B., 9
Russell, Nina Ryan, 239

Sanders, Hattie Belle, 241
Sanders Oscar Haywood, 194, 241-42
Sanders, Robert, 23
Sapp, Marvin, 75
Saunders, Alberta Brockington, 243
Saunders, Mary J., 245
Saunders, Monroe Randolph Jr., 57
Saunders, Monroe Randolph Sr., 39, 53, 57, 243-44
Saunders, Willard E., 245
Scheppe, John, 2
Schooler, Alexander Robinson, 8, 135, 162, 169, 223, 246-47
Schultz, David, 248
Scott, Phillip Lee, 70, 249, 262
Sears, Lena, 203, 250
Selassie, Halie, 189
Seymour, William J., 1, 15, 165, 221

Shelton, Geneva, 251
Shelton, Nehemiah, 32, 253
Shelton, Omega Y. L., 32, 253
Shelton, Samuel McDowell, 32, 150, 252-253
Shields, Judge Pierce (J. P.), 33
Shields, Waddell P., 33
Shouse, Edward E., 50
Showell, Cornelius, 48
Showell, Genevieve Francis, 254
Showell, Winfield Amos, 46, 49, 84, 245, 254-55
Singleton, Alfred, 44, 256
Smith, Albart, 25, 41, 87, 265
Smith, Elias D., 25, 87, 219
Smith, Francis Leonard, 10, 53, 257
Smith, Helen, 58, 258
Smith, Horace, 11
Smith, Josephine Anne, 259
Smith, Karl Franklin, 9, 86, 149, 176, 257, 259-60
Smith, Willie Mae Ford, 261-262
Snow, Wallace, 14,
Solomon, Frank S., 53, 263
Spencer, Helen Lee, 264
Spencer, Hubert J., 21, 23, 93, 264
Stokes, Carl B., 280
Stokes, Cleveland H., 25, 41, 219, 265-266, 297
Sturtevant, William, 197
Sunday, Billy, 164

Taylor, Marshall, 267
Temple, Horace, 268
Tobin, Robert Franklin, 147, 260, 269
Tolbert, Lambert Roosevelt, 107, 270

Turpin, Joseph Morsel, 8, 34, 85, 122, 129, 191, 208, 226, 246, 254, 271-72
Turpin, Ruth Beatrice, 226, 271
Tutu, Desmond, 143
Twyman, Harrison, 66, 77, 273
Tyson, James Edison, 274
Tyson, Betty Showell, 274, 275-276

Urshan, Andrew David, 167, 239
Urshan, Nathaniel A., 53

Varnell, A. F., 9
Wagner, Norman Leonard, 11, 274, 277-78
Wagner, Rita H., 277
Waller, Thomas (Fats), 191, 198
Walsh, Charles Constantine, 137, 279
Walsh, Christine Agatha, 137, 279
Washington, Joel G., 37, 38, 289
Watkins, Charles W., 280
Watkins, Sherman, 50, 68
Watson, John S., 39, 57, 137
Watson, Samuel, 271
Wauls, Robert Allen, 281
Weathers, Joseph, 29, 53, 66, 282
Weeks, Gwendolyn G., 11
Weeks, Thomas John, 283-84
White, George, 279, 285
White, Melvina E., 39, 285-86
Wilder, Douglas, 78
Wiley, George H., 14, 55
Wilkes, C. R., 83
Williams, Frank W., 15, 17, 287-288
Williams, Joseph David, 22, 37, 289

Williams, McKinley, 46, 49, 179, 291-292
Williams, Smallwood Edmond, 21, 22, 46, 53, 112, 142, 185, 293-296
Williams, Verna Lucille, 185, 294

Williams, Wallace, 294, 295
Wilson, Quander Lear, 41, 50, 266, 297-298

Young, Elzie William, 44, 89, 299

Index of Organizations and Congregations

African Methodist Episcopal Church, 155

African Methodist Episcopal Zion Church, 261

Alliance of Apostolic Churches of Christ Jesus, 65

Apostle Church of Christ in God, 14, 35-36, 55, 60, 132, 209, 233

Apostolic Assemblies of Christ, 59, 95, 210

Apostolic Church of Christ, 14, 194, 286

Apostolic Church of God, 103

Apostolic Faith Assembly (Columbus), 21, 187, 259

Apostolic Faith Assembly (Indianapolis), 7, 83, 160, 168, 225, 269

Apostolic Faith Assembly (Philadelphia), 122, 155, 183, 271

Apostolic Faith Home Assembly, 97, 99, 117, 133, 135, 176

Apostolic Faith Mission Church of God, 15, 16, 288

Apostolic Inter-Organizational Fellowship Conference, 53, 169, 295

Apostolic Overcoming Holy Church of God, 17, 19, 81, 221, 235, 288 *see* Ethiopian Overcoming Holy Church of God,

Belvedere Gospel Tabernacle, 97, 99

Beth-El Churches of Christ, 43, 69, 101, 140

Bethel United Way of the Cross Church of Christ, 77

Bethel United Church of Jesus Christ Apostolic (UK), 138

Bethesda Church of Christ, 46, 88

Bible Way Church (Washington, DC), 21, 46, 53, 112, 251

Bible Way Church of Our Lord Jesus Christ World Wide, 23, 46-48, 63, 189, 254, 293

Bible Way Pentecostal Apostolic Church, 49

Cainhoy Miracle Revival Center, 58, 258

Christ Temple (Indianapolis), 7, 44, 147, 166, 168, 205

Christian Faith Band, 13, 35, 133, 135, 188

Church in the Lord Jesus Christ, 173

Church of the Lord Jesus Christ, 22, 31-32, 56, 179, 173, 252

Church of God in Christ, 1, 39, 95, 105, 115, 208, 214

Church of God in Christ#6, 243

Church of God (Apostolic), 13-14, 35, 49, 60, 123, 233, 261

Church of Our Lord Jesus Christ, 8, 21-24, 31, 34, 46, 49, 63, 142, 174, 188

DC, Delaware, and Maryland District Council, 84, 113, 245

Eastern District Council, 84, 105, 122, 156, 197, 208, 246, 272

Emmanuel Tabernacle Baptist Church Apostolic, 19-20, 153, 204, 228

Ethiopian Overcoming Holy Church, *see* Apostolic Overcoming Holy Church of God, 17, 221, 288
Evangelistic Churches of Christ of the Apostolic, 63, 179
First Apostolic Faith Church, 10, 47, 85, 114, 196, 237, 255
Free Gospel Church of the Apostles' Doctrine, 52, 67, 152

Glorious Church of God in Christ, 17, 25-26, 41, 87, 153, 219
Grace Apostolic Church, 147, 267
Greater Bethlehem Temple (Clinton Street), 44, 84, 121, 124, 195, 256
Greater Morning Star Apostolic Church, 71, *see* Morning Star Pentecostal Church, 113

Higher Ground Always Abounding Assemblies, 50, 68
Highway Christian Church of Christ, 34, 43, 53, 66, 208, 254
Highway Churches of Christ, 43, 69, 128, 140
Holy Temple Church of the Lord Jesus Christ, 32, 56, 150

International Bible Way Church of Jesus Christ, 48, 210, 211

Jamaica Union of Apostolic Churches, 285, 286

King's Apostle Holy Church, 271
King's Chapel Assembly, 191, 197

Lincoln Park Church of Christ, 118, 187, 280

Lively Stone Church of God, 210, 249
Living Witnesses of the Apostolic Faith, Inc., 54-55, 224

Mayfield Apostolic Holiness Church, 204
Morning Star Pentecostal Church, 71, 113
Mount Hebron Apostolic Temple of Our Lord Jesus Christ, 55
Mt. Zion Apostolic Church, 45, 199

National Apostolic Fellowship Association, 67, 132, 152

Original Glorious Church of God in Christ, 25, 41-42, 50, 87, 159, 220, 266

Pentecostal Assemblies of Jesus Christ, 9, 10, 156, 170, 242, 248, 260
Pentecostal Assemblies of the World, 7-12, 29, 39, 44, 47, 126, 155, 166, 208, 246, 257, 271, 277
Pentecostal Churches of the Apostolic Faith, 10, 44-45, 89, 161, 195, 203, 256, 299
Pentecostal Ministerial Alliance, 161, 170
Pentecostal Followers of Jesus Christ, 196
Progressive Church of the Lord Jesus Christ, 23, 37-38, 289

Redeemed Assembly of Jesus Christ, Apostolic, 34, 66
Refuge Temple Assemblies of Yahweh, 23, 53, 61, 64, 215

Rehoboth Church of God in Christ Jesus Apostolic, 39, 85, 116

Shiloh Apostolic Church, 137, 279
Shiloh Apostolic Temple Church, Inc., 35, 67, 132
Sixteenth Baptist Church, 235

Temple Church of Christ, 188, 191, 193
The Churches of God and True Holiness, 27-28, 65, 145
Triumph the Church and Kingdom of God in Christ, 1, 25, 87, 219, 265

United Church of Jesus Christ (Apostolic), 39, 53, 57, 243
United Pentecostal Church International, 181
United Way of the Cross Churches of Christ, 29, 63-64, 77, 273
Universal Church of Christ, 103

Way Back to Pentecost Church, 268
Way of the Cross Church of Christ, 22, 29-30, 67, 109, 111, 139, 152

Zion Gospel Churches of the Apostolic Faith, 33

Index of Terms

Aenon Bible College, 10, 98, 148, 156, 176, 207, 259, 275
Aenon School of Theology and Bible College, 176
American University, 171
Arroyo Seco Camp Meeting, 2, 99
Azusa Street Revival, 1, 7, 15, 97, 99, 159, 157, 165, 197, 221, 287

Baltimore Ohio Railroad (B&O Railroad), 129
Bethune-Cookman College, 252
Bonnie Brae Street Prayer Meeting, 15, 287
Brotherhood of Sleeping Car Porters, 129
Butler University, 147, 205

Carnegie Hall, 185
Church of Christ Bible Institute, 21, 119, 188
Civil Rights Movement, 129, 221, 235, 280
Columbia University, 191
Coppin State College, 101, 276

DeBarge Family, 75

Ethiopian World Federation, 189

Finished Work of Calvary, 133

Great Depression, 95, 103, 160, 250, 268

Harvard University, 283
Holiness Movement, 1, 105, 271

Howard University, 140, 141, 146, 185, 243

Interfaith Council of Religions, 295
International Women's Council (COOLJC), 22, 216

lynching/lynched, 226, 241, 272

Moody Bible Institute, 103, 191, 201, 212
Morgan State College, 200, 254

National Association for the Advancement of Colored People (NAACP), 139, 235, 255
National Pentecostal Young People's Union (PAW), 10, 75, 148
Negro National League, 269
Northwestern Theological Seminary, 115

R. C. Lawson Library, 94,
Racism, 23, 165, 189, 280
Rutgers University, 213, 252

Samuel K. Grimes Child Welfare Center, 156, 171
slave/slaves, 13, 86, 114, 123, 219
Social Justice, Economic and Racial Equality Commission, 23
Southern Christian Leadership Conference, 25
Stellar Gospel Music Awards, 278

Union Theological Seminary, 91

Work Progress Administration (WPA), 250

Xavier University, 100

Youth For Christ, 141

About the Author

Apostle Cornelius Showell was called into the Kingdom for such a time as this as a man destined to empower the masses through his prolific preaching and teaching. His passion for the Kingdom and the things of God and compassion for men and women's souls have made him sought after to preach good tidings proclaim liberty to the meek and captive.

After receiving the mantle from his father, the Honorable Bishop Winfield Amos Showell, in 1987, he became the senior pastor of, one of the oldest Apostolic churches in the United States, The First Apostolic Faith Church of Jesus Christ, International in Baltimore.

A noted Baltimore entrepreneur and businessman, for over 30 years, Showell has been involved in various real estate and commercial endeavors as a manager, developer, and owner. In keeping with his noted care for the senior citizens of Baltimore, his ventures include the development of two multi-unit housing complexes for the elderly.

A scholar of African American history, he was the founding executive director of the Maryland Commission on Negro History and Culture, taught African American Studies at Morgan State University for numerous years, and was instrumental in establishing AFRAM, Baltimore City's highly acclaimed African American Heritage Festival.

In 2002, Showell was consecrated to the Apostleship by the Executive Board of Bishops of the Bible Way Church of our Lord Jesus Christ, Incorporated. He served as Presiding Bishop and Chief Apostle of International Bible Way Church of Jesus Christ, Inc. from 2006-2014. As such he provided guidance to over 500 pastors and several affiliate organizations heads through his wisdom and leadership.

Apostle Showell is married to the love of his life, the Elect Lady Augusta Showell. They have three sons, Byron, Andre, and Cornelius, II.

www.ingramcontent.com/pod-product-compliance
Lightning Source LLC
Chambersburg PA
CBHW070046080526
44586CB00013B/936